LOVE NEVER FAILS

Bishop Donald Hying

Love Never Fails

*Living the Catholic Faith
in Our Daily Lives*

IGNATIUS PRESS   SAN FRANCISCO

Cover art:
Christ Washing the Apostles' Feet
Giotto di Bondone
Scrovegni Chapel, Padua, Italy
© Cameraphoto Arte, Venice/Art Resource, New York

Cover design by Enrique J. Aguilar

ISBN 978-1-62164-407-1 (PB)
ISBN 978-1-64229-164-3 (eBook)
Library of Congress Catalogue Number 2020946600
Printed in the United States of America ∞

CONTENTS

PREFACE

I love the idea that my life is a romantic adventure, a marriage of my soul to God, that my days and years are a gradual unfolding of the Lord and me growing ever more comfortable with each other, that the meaning of my life is mysteriously eternal and knowingly transparent in the immediacy of the present moment.

We live in an exciting moment in history as the Church throughout the world feels the energy and the urgency of the New Evangelization. Catholics everywhere are asking themselves the same questions: How can I live my faith with greater authenticity and commitment? How can I lead those who have fallen away from the faith back to the Church? How can I help to heal the poverty, violence, and suffering of the world? How can my parish be more effective and dynamic? This book hopes to support that seeking for a deeper communion with the Lord and His Church together.

Part I

God's Love for Us Is
Sacramental and Personal

Self-Surrender to the Transforming Love of God

During a retreat I was on years ago, the director posed the question, is it harder to love God or be loved by God? At the time, I thought it's harder to love God because of all the effort it takes to be holy, prayerful, virtuous, and focused. As the years of my life have flown by, however, I now think it is harder to be loved by God. To let God love me demands a surrender, a docility, and a humility. It also means that I am challenged to see myself as loveable—no easy feat.

In my years of priestly ministry, I have discovered that many people do not really love themselves or even like who they see in the mirror. On some levels this fact makes sense. No one knows us as we know ourselves; no one else sees all of our temptations, bad thoughts, sins, and messiness as we do. To live with oneself one's whole life is at times a tremendous burden.

Is this struggle part of the original flaw of Original Sin, when Adam and Eve mistakenly thought that eating the forbidden fruit would make their lives happier and more fulfilling, when actually everything was already perfect in the first place? In many ways, it is easier to stay in my fortress of aloneness, walled off from the love of God and others, because then I do not have to wrestle with my sense of unworthiness, shame, and guilt.

The joyful news of our faith is that God finds us loveable, even irresistible! In the Person of Jesus Christ, He comes in passionate pursuit of us, seeking to attract and draw us into the sacred marriage bond between Jesus and the Church. When we surrender to this divine initiative, we discover our lives to be a sacred romance, a passionate love relationship that spills out into everyone and everything we encounter.

When people are in love, they glow. They long to be with their beloved, offer extravagant gifts, suffer inconvenience, and embrace sacrifice, all in order to demonstrate the love in their hearts. All of that passionate purpose can be unleashed in us when we truly experience in our heads and hearts the unconditional, infinite, fiery, and eternal love of God. As the saying goes, "God loves you, and there is nothing you can do about it!"

When I took a promise of celibacy as a transitional deacon in 1988, I, at least, had enough insight to grasp that a lifetime of experience would be required for me truly to understand what such a commitment actually means.

Celibacy is more than a simple renunciation of marriage and family or even exclusive friendships; it is the opposite of shutting love out of life. Rather, celibacy requires a generous, open, and sacrificial stance of love to all people—an availability to the beauty, suffering, and needs of everyone. Gradually coming to allow God's love deeper into my life has freed me to live this celibate stance with greater understanding and purpose, knowing that the divine love of the Lord is the only reality that will satisfy the restless longings and desires of my human heart. Letting myself be loved by God as well as being nourished by the Eucharist, forgiven of my sins, and called to His holy purpose liberates me to love others without conditions, possessiveness, or expectations. By no means have I arrived at perfection, but with the passage of years, I feel less need for affirmation, attention, and affection from others. God gradually becomes enough for me.

The reflections offered here on celibacy apply to all of us in different ways, whether married, single, or widowed. By virtue of our life in Christ, baptized as beloved children of the Father, we all have the same journey to make, the path of self-surrender whereby we open ourselves in freedom and humility to the transforming love of God.

The first step, to which we must return again and again, is allowing God to love us, letting Him break through our walls of shame, guilt, and self-loathing. This spiritual breakthrough frees us to love parents, children, spouses, family, parishioners, friends, and strangers without conditions, limits, or expectation.

Kairos Moments

Perhaps the greatest obstacle to our spiritual growth today is the intense and relentless busyness that pervades our days. Between work, school, sports, meetings, and social commitments, life can easily be a treadmill of ceaseless activity where we are simply rushing to get the next thing done. Silence, rest, prayer, and leisure are absolutely necessary if we truly seek to be in deeper communion with God, others, and our deepest selves.

Understanding this need, Catholicism has always called people to days and seasons of prayer and celebration. Sundays, holy days, retreats, and festive octaves are sacred times when we step out of the world of work and action into God's time and space—the place of holy Sabbath. Remember, even God rested on the seventh day.

The ancient Greeks had two words for "time"—*chronos* and *kairos*. *Chronos* time is the sequential unfolding of hours and days—the world of schedules, work, and tasks. When you go to work or school on a Monday morning and it seems as if you have been there for hours already, then you look at the clock and it is 9:07 A.M.—that is *chronos* time!

Kairos time represents those transcendent experiences that lift us beyond and out of ourselves and we lose track of

This is a modified version of an article previously published as "God Waits Lovingly for Us in the 'Kairos' Moments of Our Daily Life", *Northwest Indiana Catholic* (website), accessed September 8, 2020, https://www.nwicatholic.com /index.php/2011-10-28-15-52-16/bishop-hying-column/2887-god-waits -lovingly-for-us-in-the-kairos-moments-of-our-daily-life.

time altogether. Playing outside on a long summer night, celebrating at a party with our best friends, and deeply communing with our spouse are such moments—the passage of five hours feels like just a few minutes. God lives in *kairos* time, the eternal moment of now, so the Eucharist is an experience of the timeless life of Heaven, where we will be seated at the Supper of the Lamb, loving and praising God, in complete union with each other. Mass prepares our hearts to learn how to love God in the sacrament of the present moment.

Think of chapter 10 of the Gospel of Luke where Mary is simply sitting at the feet of Jesus, attentive and listening, while Martha is running around in the kitchen. Jesus does not rebuke Martha for working hard at necessary tasks, but calls her to see the deeper purpose of a dinner party. What is the point of having a beautiful table and delicious food, if stress and distraction keep us from enjoying the guests?

In order to be effective in what I do, I need *kairos* moments each day. So I try to spend some time each day doing absolutely nothing productive. Whether I sit in my rocking chair and look out the window, go for a walk and watch the sunset, lie down on my bed and think, or ride my bike, I need such experiences to refocus on the presence of God and my own humanity. If all of my life is action, if I am simply consumed by doing, I become spiritually dull. Wasting time every day is important in a world that demands that we do more and more. I can easily put prayer on the back burner because there are so many tasks to be accomplished, so much mail on my desk, so many activities on my schedule—but what is the point of such ceaseless activity if I am not spending time with the Lord in prayer and taking some time simply to be and not do?

God is waiting for us in the *kairos* moments.

Vulnerable Real Presence

While doing seminary formation work, I would often emphasize the importance of "presence" with the seminarians—the significance of being available, visible, and vulnerable in ministry. As a priest, I would tell them, sometimes you will get a hospital call at two o'clock in the morning, which will summon you to the bedside of a dying parishioner. You will get out of your warm bed, groggy with sleep, drive across town, and engage with some people who are scared and sad as they look death in the face; they will be looking to you for consolation and strength in this difficult moment. You do not need to give them a theological treatise on the Resurrection of Christ! What they will remember is the fact that you were there and cared about them. They will also remember if you were not there.

How *often* we crave the simple physical presence of people whom we love and who love us. They don't have to say anything profound or do anything heroic. We just feel better when we are around them and know that somehow everything is going to be alright when they are with us. We also miss them when we are separated from each other.

Jesus knew this very profound human need and desire, so He gave us the Eucharist. In this Real Presence of Christ in the Blessed Sacrament, we enjoy the fullness of the presence of God. The Lord is fully with us—accompanying us in the simple form of bread and wine, becoming food for our souls and a consoling companion for our earthly pilgrimage.

Just as Jesus makes the invisible God visible for us in human form, so too the Eucharist is Jesus' way of being accessible to our human senses through the sight, sounds, taste, smell, and feeling of the Mass and Holy Communion. In the Eucharist, we see the sacramental reality of divine love, made manifest for us. God also becomes fully available to us through the Word of the Scriptures, the grace of the sacraments, the refreshment of prayer, and the divine indwelling in our souls. God is not a remote, distant deity far away from us, but is right here, accessible and engaged in the details of our lives.

In Jesus, we also encounter the vulnerability of God. By becoming fully human, Jesus enters into the glory and tragedy, joy and suffering, of our existence in this world. In a sense, He trades the safety of Heaven for the pain and risk of the human project. We see this vulnerability in the helpless baby in Bethlehem; the healer hemmed in and jostled by eager crowds; the hostile forces that seek to hurl Him over the cliff of Nazareth; the humble one kneeling on the floor, washing feet; the scourged and tortured figure on the Cross.

God's power manifests itself as weakness and humility as well as vulnerability by being able to be hurt and even killed. Do we not see such vulnerability in the Eucharist? The transcendent God, whom the universe cannot contain, is fully present in a piece of bread and a sip from a cup. When we receive the Host in our hands, how much more powerless and simple could God possibly become? He enters our lives as food consumed.

Our experience of the Eucharist invites us to imitate the mystery that we receive as a gift. How beautiful and difficult it is to be fully present to the people with whom we are with! To appreciate the gift of the other person, to truly listen with our heart, to not be distracted with thoughts of future plans, to not be in a hurry to rush away, requires a discipline of the heart and soul. We have all seen a couple eating in a restaurant, not saying a word to each other through a whole meal, but both busily texting people who are somewhere else. Be present to the present.

The Eucharist calls us to availability, to let ourselves be inconvenienced and our schedules rearranged, to not always insist on our way of doing things, to be sensitive to the needs and feelings of others, to respond sometimes before we are even asked or compelled to do so. I've always wanted people to bother me, to ask for things, to show me their needs and their wounds. I may not always be able to help in every situation, but I want to. Jesus asks us to be available to and affected by the terrible suffering of the world.

Our Christian faith invites us to be vulnerable, to love courageously even when we are rejected and hurt by those to whom we open our hearts, and to share our faith and our feelings, our heart and our thoughts, even when we are not understood or such vulnerability is not reciprocated. To love and give, even when our efforts go unnoticed and unappreciated, is to taste even now the glorious and terrible love of Jesus Crucified, the One whose stance toward us is radically unconditional and generously favorable, the One who is always fully present with us. What a relief to know that we do not always have to be in charge, in control, and running the show. When we have the courage to show our own weakness, struggle, and even sin—that is, to be vulnerable—so often we are graced with understanding, encouragement, acceptance, and even mercy.

Everything Is a Gift from the Father

One of my favorite authors is G. K. Chesterton, a convert to Catholicism and an insightfully witty author. He wrote much on the mystery and wonder of life, concluding that our existence in this world is both mystical and magical. He spoke often of gratitude, the intuitive response to the Giver of all gifts when we realize the enormity of what we have received from the hands of God. We know, as Christians, that thankfulness is a way of life and the vision of understanding the world.

When I contemplate my life—the beauty, truth, and goodness that surround me every day—my heart over-flows with gratitude. I thank God for the big things—the mercy and love of the Lord, the promise of salvation and forgiveness, the presence of Jesus and the Church, the gift of the Scriptures and the sacraments, the friendship of the saints. I thank Him for my family and friends, the people who show me kindness and love beyond anything I ever deserve or even dare to ask for. I am enormously grateful for the call to the priesthood and the extraordinary privi-lege of serving as a bishop. All of it is a gift—undeserved, unearned, and unexpected.

I also thank the Lord for the "little" things—meals shared with friends; books to read; pilgrimages to beautiful places; exercise at the gym; a bed to sleep in; work to do;

This is a modified version of an article previously published as "We Are Called to Give Thanks and Praise to the Bounteous Giver of All Gifts", *Northwest Indiana Catholic* (website), accessed September 15, 2020, https://www.nwi catholic.com/index.php/2011-10-28-15-52-16/bishop-hying-column?start=153.

warm clothes to wear in the winter; sunsets and clouds; birds in the sky; the joy of walking down a country road on a summer's day. It's easy to take our life for granted, to stop seeing the wonders and miracles that surround us, to focus on what we don't have rather than what we have been given, to view the problems and difficulties more than the blessings and the gifts, to look at what is wrong rather than what is so gloriously right.

Gratitude saves us from self-pity, resentment, jealousy, anger, selfishness, and entitlement. Thankfulness sets us free to be generous, joyful, kind, and sacrificial, because we know that everything we have is a gift, meant to be shared and passed on to others. When I can embrace the mystery, wonder, and beauty that surround me, I realize that all of us act out the drama of our lives on a far bigger stage than we can dare to imagine, for we are all players in God's big love story, and that is where Jesus comes in.

Jesus came to earth to share freely with us the bounty of the Father's love. He fed, taught, healed, and forgave thousands of people, not because they deserved or earned it, but precisely because they didn't. His whole life was a gift of God to the human race—the radical and profound gift of self, poured out in the Son becoming flesh. Jesus' big miracles and the unrecorded kindnesses, His thunderous preaching and benevolent laughter, His feeding of the five thousand and the intimate dinners with friends, the foot washing and the Eucharist, and finally His suffering and death on the Cross are all divine gifts, not only for the people of that time, but also for us.[1]

Jesus gifts us every day with a new opportunity, a fresh start to live our limited days in imitation of His gracious

---

[1] See Mt 14:13–21; Mk 6:30–44; Lk 9:10–17; Jn 6:1–15; Lk 10:38–42; Jn 13:1–20; Mt 17:32–50; Mk 15:33–39; Lk 23:26–49, and Jn 19:17–28.

generosity. Each moment of our lives contains within itself the tantalizing fingerprints of God, inviting us to be joyful and grateful. One of my favorite quotes comes from Henry David Thoreau, a nineteenth-century naturalist, author, conscientious objector (he had the courage to condemn the injustice of the Mexican-American War), and social commentator. He famously said in his memoir *Walden*, "I went to the woods because I wished to live deliberately, to front only the essential facts of life, and see if I could not learn what it had to teach, and not, when I came to die, discover that I had not lived." In a letter to a friend, he also said (less famously), "I am grateful for what I am and have. My thanksgiving is perpetual."

When we have the courage to "front only the essential facts of life", we discover the fundamental truths of the universe: God created us in sheer graciousness; love is the explanation of everything; we will only know joy when we give ourselves away; Jesus calls us to a life of service and gratitude; everything is a gift from the Father. We bring all of that thankfulness and praise to the Eucharist, which comes from the Greek word that means "thanksgiving". We glorify the bounteous Giver of all gifts, the Divine "Magician" as Chesterton put it,[2] the One who pulled all of this beauty, truth, and goodness out of the divine hat and gave it to *us*.

---

[2] G.K. Chesterton, *Orthodoxy* (London: Jone Lane Company, 1908), p. 34, https://d2y1pz2y630308.cloudfront.net/15471/documents/2016/10/G.K.Chesterton-Orthodoxy.pdf.

Christ Waits for Us

The Sacrament of Reconciliation is a profound experience of healing, forgiveness, and liberation in which the Lord frees us of our sins and calls us to deeper conversion. Reconciliation is at the very heart of our faith, for the Lord Jesus' fundamental mission is to reconcile us to the Father, to one another, and to our truest deepest selves.

He accomplishes this reconciliation in three essential ways.

Through the Incarnation, by assuming our flesh, Jesus unites the fullness of God's divinity with the fullness of our humanity. In His very Person, the Lord is already healing the chasm between God and us that sin creates. In His ministry, Jesus eats with sinners, lets prostitutes anoint His feet, proclaims mercy to the lost, and heals those marginalized by sickness and disease. Finally, in His death and Resurrection, the Lord definitively breaks the power of sin and death, creating a path for us to journey to the Father's house, free from the power of fear and evil.

Baptism is the primary Sacrament of Reconciliation, which joins us to the life of the Trinity and washes our sins away in the waters made holy by the Paschal Mystery of Christ and the presence of the Spirit.

The Sacrament of Reconciliation renews us in that baptismal innocence, freeing us to begin again on the road to conversion. I try to celebrate the Sacrament of Reconciliation once a month, because the experience of sacramental forgiveness renews and strengthens my faith, frees me of my sins, and calls me to deeper conversion and sincere effort to be holy as God is holy.

Many Catholics do not regularly celebrate the sacrament, perhaps because of negative experiences from the past, a reluctance to speak of one's failures and sins to another, lack of catechesis and formation, or simply a perception that it is unnecessary to go to Confession. Experiencing the dynamic of the sacrament from both sides of the confessional screen, I personally testify that regular sacramental reconciliation is one of the best practices we can embrace to find peace, joy, love, mercy, and forgiveness.

In chapter 20 of the Gospel of John, Jesus appears to the Apostles on Easter Sunday night through locked doors, wishing them peace, breathing the Holy Spirit on them, and commissioning them to go forth and proclaim forgiveness with authority to absolve sins in His name. Seemingly, Jesus could not wait to come back from the dead in order to share with everyone the reconciling fruits of His death and Resurrection. Both this Scripture passage and the practice of the Church from the beginning teach us that Reconciliation in Christ is a communal experience, that Jesus loves and forgives us most profoundly through the mediating power of the Church. So, even if I am confessing privately to a priest, I am doing so within the whole community, because the priest represents both Christ and the Church.

I grew up in a family of six boys, so my parents had some basic rules to survive our childhood, one of which was to not throw things in the living room. One day, when I was about four, I was watching television and minding my own business when one of my brothers came into the room and threw a ball to me, which I instinctively threw back. It hit and smashed one of my mother's porcelain vases, which shattered into dozens of pieces. At that age,

I had not read the book of Genesis yet, but I immediately did what Adam and Eve did after they sinned; I ran upstairs and hid under my bed. When my mother confronted me with the deed, I then imitated Adam perfectly by pointing the finger at my brother as the true culprit!

I share that childhood memory because it teaches me some very important things. When I disobey God, refuse to listen to Him, and move away from our relationship, life shatters into pieces, like my mother's vase. We live in a world of such violence, rage, conflict, and hatred. Our lives often feel like a jumble of broken pieces that we are trying to put back together.

The good news of Jesus' reconciling mercy is that we can't fix it alone and we don't even have to try. The Lord wants to do it in us. That's where the sacraments come in.

I also learned that our human, instinctive response to moments of moral failure is to hide from God and pass blame to others. Reconciliation calls me from the darkness into the light and invites me to claim my own sin, not to shame or humiliate me, but to free me from guilt, sadness, and fear.

If you regularly celebrate the Sacrament of Reconciliation, you know how healing the experience is, spiritually, psychologically, and emotionally. If you don't regularly confess, I invite you to try it, once a month for a year. Then take an assessment. Ask yourself if you are more peaceful and joyful. Does the loving and merciful presence of God seem more real and close? Have you grown in your mastery over habitual sins, negative attitudes, and spiritual malaise? In this powerful sacrament, the Lord gives us extraordinary graces to grow in our love for the Lord and let Him heal the broken pieces of our lives and world. Try it. You will come to love Confession. Christ is waiting for us with open, merciful arms.

God Is Drawn to Our Weakness

Several years ago, I was blessed to lead a spiritual pilgrimage to France, one of my favorite places. We visited sites associated with great saints, like Saint Margaret Mary at Paray-le-Monial, Saint John Vianney at Ars, Saints Francis de Sales and Jane Frances de Chantal at Annecy, Saint Vincent de Paul at Paris, Saint Thérèse of Lisieux, and Saint Joan of Arc at Rouen.

We also went to Lourdes, the beautiful shrine of healing, nestled in the Pyrenees mountains. Highlights there included celebrating a Mass in the grotto at 6:00 A.M. with a full moon shining, participating in the Rosary candlelight procession, going into the baths, and climbing up to the fortress that overlooks the town.

The most compelling and moving part of Lourdes is the vast number of people who are suffering a wide variety of illnesses, maladies, and disabilities. They come to this remote French town in the tens of thousands, triumphing over obstacles and enduring discomforts just to get there. As pilgrims, they have come to pray and to bathe in the waters of the spring that the Virgin Mary had instructed Saint Bernadette to discover in 1858.

Most will not find a physical healing, although thousands have over the years, but they will come away with a deeper experience of God's love for them, a stronger resolve to bear the cross of their suffering, and a deeper peace that comes from acceptance and surrender. One of

the things that strikes me about Lourdes is that the sick
and disabled receive preferential treatment in the baths,
processions, Masses, and walkways of the shrine. They are
the most important people there.

Such a practice is a startling inverse of how often the
world is, where the powerful, beautiful, and elite receive
pride of place.

Lourdes is a profound incarnation of the Catholic conviction that Christ comes to us in the disguise of the poor,
the sick, and the weak and awaits our merciful response
through them. An attendant at the baths drove this point
home to me, as I awaited my turn to go in, saying, with
tears in his eyes, that his work at Lourdes was a privilege,
as it allowed him to bathe and care for the Body of Christ
on a daily basis. This holy shrine is a divinely chosen site
where the fullness of human weakness and suffering con-
verge in a startling fashion with the fullness of God's merciful and healing power.

It may be tempting at times to wish to live in a world
completely free of suffering, poverty, weakness, and illness, yet would that be a good thing? Obviously, in the
name of the merciful Christ, we seek to eradicate disease,
malnutrition, unemployment, and homelessness, but we
can never fully escape the Cross. As maddening as that may
be on a human level, could it be that we all need some
form of suffering to humanize us?

If I were completely self-sufficient, living with no need-
iness, weakness, or dependency, I would be tempted to
shut myself off from other people and maybe even God
Himself. Suffering in those we love opens up deep reser-
voirs of compassion in us, as our own inadequacies compel
us to reach out to others. How often in our lives has a
harsh encounter with the Cross led us to a deeper faith,
prayer, and awareness of our radical need for God?

Societies that do not tolerate human weakness and imperfection often end up eliminating those who do not measure up to some mythical standard of sufficiency. The Third Reich comes to mind. Our rich Catholic spirituality and theology of suffering can deeply inform and shape our national debate on end-of-life issues, euthanasia, and health care. Saint John Paul's 1984 apostolic letter on the meaning of human suffering, *Salvifici Doloris*, serves as a foundational document to deepen our understanding of how God and our human weakness intersect in Jesus Christ.

Lourdes reminds us that we do not have to be perfect, strong, healthy, and beautiful to be loveable; that God actually finds our "disabilities" to be attractive; that He is drawn to our weakness; and that our sin arouses his compassion. Ted Turner famously said that Christianity is for losers.[1] I could not agree more. Only those who have lost their self-sufficient pride and know they need a savior can find the Crucified and Risen One who can heal, forgive, and love us into eternal life.

[1] Turner made the comment in 1990 in a speech to the American Humanist Association, an atheist convention.

Spiritual Spendthrifts

Imagine being awakened in the middle of the night by the smell of smoke. In fear you dash to touch your bedroom door; it is fiery hot. Plumes of choking smoke are already pouring in from the hallway. Your only means of escape is to jump from the second-floor window, but when you open the sash, you stand there frozen, unable to move.

You have only a few moments to save your life, but you cannot do it. Just then, when all seems lost, a firefighter breaks into the room and bodily throws you out the window to a safety net on the ground.

The next day, you learn that the brave firefighter who saved your life was himself overcome by smoke inhalation and died in the flames. How would you feel about this man? Would you go to his funeral? How would you remember him? How will your life be different?

I often use this story to explain the power of salvation won for us through the Cross and Resurrection of Christ. In the terror of the Crucifixion, Jesus literally trades His life for ours, entering into the dark night of death in order to offer us eternal life.

This is a modified version of an article originally published as "Choking in the Deadly Grasp of Sin, Jesus in Breaks, Wraps Us in His Net of Grace and Mercy", *Northwest Indiana Catholic* (website), March 20, 2016, https://www.nwicatholic.com/index.php/2011-10-28-15-52-16/bishop-hying-column/3495-choking-in-the-deadly-grasp-of-sin-jesus-in-breaks-wraps-us-in-his-net-of-grace-and-mercy.

When all seemed lost, when humanity was trapped in the choking deadly grasp of sin, Jesus breaks into human history and wraps us in the safety net of grace and mercy.

In the story above, the sacrifice of the firefighter perhaps buys you a few more decades of life on earth. As great as that is, it pales to nothingness in comparison to the glory of eternal life with the Triune God in the Kingdom of Heaven.

When we contemplate the infinite value of such a gift, purchased for us through the precious blood of the Son, our sense of gratitude for the saving death and glorious rising of Jesus Christ knows no bounds!

For many Christians, John 3:16–17 encapsulates the core of our faith in Christ. "For God so loved the world that he gave his only-begotten Son, that whoever believes in him should not perish but have eternal life. For God sent the Son into the world, not to condemn the world, but that the world might be saved through him." You see the first verse of this Scripture passage held up on placards at sporting events, you find it in parish mission statements, and you read it in evangelical tracts left at your door.

John 3:16 reminds us that God loves us enough to send the Son in order to save us for all eternity. How precious our souls must be to the Lord! God could have saved us any way that He pleased. Yet in the Cross, we see the Son embracing the hardest path imaginable for the sake of our salvation.

Maybe God lets us feel at times the terrifying abyss of life without Him so that we have some experience against which to measure the value of salvation. When we sin and shut God out, when we suffer and feel abandoned, or when we just experience normal bouts of loneliness and misunderstanding, we get little glimpses of what Hell would be.

How can I ever really know the joy of salvation unless I lift my experiences of anxiety, dread, sin, and isolation to God on the Cross? Can I really appreciate the gift of my life in Christ until I have somehow been painfully uprooted from my complacent self-sufficiency? As Saint Augustine puts it, "For a clean heart to be created, the unclean one must be crushed."[1]

In the last year of her life, Saint Thérèse of Lisieux endured the death agonies of her tuberculosis along with a deep spiritual darkness that left her doubting her vocational choice as a nun, her personal salvation, the reality of Heaven, and even the existence of God.

Through it all, she kept faith, clung to the Cross, and trusted Jesus' promise of salvation. Could it be that God was purifying Thérèse's remarkable love through this dark night? Can the same be true for us?

Once we have tasted the darkness and the light, sensed separation from God and unity with Him, felt the emptiness of Good Friday and the presence of Easter Sunday, we know the weight and value of salvation in a way that transforms our minds, hearts, souls, and bodies.

When we have a real sense of from what we have been saved and a living experience of for whom we have been saved, thanksgiving and praise become the themes of our prayer. We can never give back to God what He has lavished upon us, so we humbly accept the saving gift and live only to pass the Crucified and Risen Christ on to others. We become spiritual spendthrifts, like Mary of Bethany, who spent three hundred days' wages to anoint Jesus' feet with a pound of aromatic nard.[2]

---

[1] Office of Readings, Sunday of Week 14, "From the sermon by Saint Augustine, Bishop" (Serm. 19, 2–3: CCL 41, 252–54), http://www.liturgies .net/Liturgies/Catholic/loh/week14sundayor.htm.

[2] See Mt 26:6–13; Mk 14:3–9; Lk 7:37–38; Jn 12:1–8.

Often, I hear complaints from people that Mass is boring or they don't get anything out of it. My consistent response is that the Eucharist is not about us! We gather to worship and thank God for the gift of Jesus Christ. Can you imagine going to the memorial service for the firefighter who saved your life and complaining it was boring?

When we approach the Eucharist with thanksgiving and humility, feeling the weight and value of the salvation offered us, our experience of the sacrament changes. We sense ourselves falling ever more deeply in love with the invisible God who reached out and grasped us from the clutches of death by dying Himself on the Cross.

Set the World on Fire for Christ

Coming from the Latin word *evangelium*, which means "gospel", evangelization simply means proclaiming the Good News of Jesus Christ to others. As Saint Paul reminds us in chapter 10 of Romans, faith comes through hearing the witness and testimony of other believers. We could also say that faith comes through seeing the example of committed Christians who act out the Gospel.

Today, we urgently need this Christian witness more than ever. According to the Center for Applied Research in the Apostolate, in 2019 on any given Sunday in America (with the exception of Easter), only 21 percent of our baptized Catholics were at Mass.[1] Imagine inviting ten guests over for dinner and only three show up. You spend the evening looking at seven empty places.

A multitude of reasons exist for this dramatic drop-off, but none justify doing nothing about it. Clearly, fewer young people find Mass compelling enough to participate in it. How we celebrate the liturgy and teach about it, as well as the quality of our preaching and our music, matter so much.

Despite the fact that we are blessed with many wonderful and dedicated catechists and teachers, we must admit that many of our people are poorly catechized. How many

---

[1] Center for Applied Research in the Apostolate, "Frequently Requested Church Statistics", 2020, https://cara.georgetown.edu/frequently-requested -church-statistics/.

Catholics can give cogent answers to the most basic questions about our faith? How many Catholics, for example, even know the most simple things, such as the four evangelists, the seven sacraments, the Ten Commandments, and the four marks of the Church? Most members of our parishes stop learning more about their faith after they are confirmed or graduate from a Catholic high school. Catechism classes and adult formation, done well both in substance and delivery, are essential.

The majority of engaged couples coming forward for marriage in the Church are not attending Mass; are cohabiting or sleeping together; are contracepting; and know very little about the faith. On top of this disturbing trend is the downward spiral of people who even want to get married at all. Marriage preparation is an opportune moment to walk with these couples; befriend them; offer them compelling formation on faith, marriage, and sexuality; and draw them into the community. Postmarriage follow-up is as important as the preparation.

I cite some of these challenges, not to be negative, not to wring my hands in despair, and not to give up, but to show some sober and challenging reasons why sharing our faith with others in a zealous, joyful, and evangelizing spirit is so absolutely needed today. I would not want to trade places with any other Catholic in history! The difficulties we face should excite and motivate us to drink deeply of the Holy Spirit and go set the world on fire for Christ.

The New Evangelization is the contemporary, robust embrace of Jesus' Great Commission given to the Apostles on the day of His Ascension in chapter 28 of Matthew's Gospel: Go into the whole world and proclaim the Gospel to every creature! From Pentecost Sunday forward, it is not so much that the Church has had a mission as it is that the mission has a Church and that mission is to announce the Good News of Jesus Christ crucified and risen to every person in the world.

Without some personal encounter with the Lord, without a deep experience of ongoing conversion as the basis of faith, catechesis can become mere history lessons and the celebration of the sacraments like empty rituals.

I will never forget a conversation with a young woman struggling with her faith who told me that Mass for her "was just a bunch of people saying a bunch of words". With the ardor of the Holy Spirit, all of our recent popes, including Francis, want to summon the vast and varied energies of the world's Catholics to this central task of witnessing Jesus to the world. How do we do that specifically? What does it look like?

Evangelization starts with the integrity and holiness of our own lives. The magnetizing power of a person in love with the Lord who perseveringly prays every day, profoundly knows the Scriptures and the *Catechism*, joyfully celebrates the sacraments, and faithfully lives the moral teachings of Christ can be extraordinary. If we practice our faith with fervor and joy, other people will be drawn to us and start asking questions and discussing their problems. Personal holiness is perennially attractive.

Secondly, we need to speak of our faith, witness to our relationship with Jesus, invite others to pray with us, encourage people to go to Mass and parish events, and talk about the love of the Lord. We do not have to knock on stranger's doors (although we probably should); simply start with the people already present in your life: relatives, friends, co-workers, and neighbors. Imagine if every one of us brought one other person to the practice of the faith, by loving them and cultivating the movement of the Spirit.

Thirdly, we need to consider our service to the poor, hungry, sick, and suffering; our love for prisoners, children, the aged, and women in crisis pregnancy; our efforts to build a world of mercy, justice, and peace—all witness powerfully to the transforming grace of faith embraced and lived. In all these ways, we make our Catholic faith visible and public because we were never meant to just let our belief in Jesus be a personal and private matter only whispered between God and each one of us alone. Jesus tells us to proclaim the Gospel from the housetops!

The Fullness of God

At the very center of our faith is the Person of Jesus Christ, whom some theologians of Vatican II name as the "Sacrament of God".[1] As Paul states in his Letter to the Colossians, Jesus "is the image of the invisible God",[2] making the fullness of the Divine Mystery present, human, known, and loved.

The Son reveals the Father and sends the Holy Spirit. In turn, the Church is the sacrament of Jesus, extending the grace, salvation, and forgiveness that flow from the Christ event, continuing the mission of eternal life inaugurated over two thousand years ago.[3]

In this context of understanding, the sacraments and worship of the Church reveal their true meaning. Through the sacraments, we receive our deepest identity as adopted children of the Father. God comes to dwell within our hearts and spirits through sanctifying grace. We receive the Holy Spirit and the forgiveness of our sins. We are fed with the Body and Blood of Christ. We are healed and sent to live the Gospel; in short, the saving fruit of Christ's victory over sin and death is extended to humanity through the sacramental actions of the Church. The sacraments keep

---

[1] Edward Schillebeeckx, O.P., *Christ, the Sacrament of the Encounter with God* (New York: Sheed and Ward, 1963), 7.

[2] Col 1:15.

[3] See Vatican Council II, Dogmatic Constitution on the Church *Lumen Gentium* (November 21, 1964), no. 1.

Jesus from simply becoming a pious memory of a good man who lived long ago.

In each sacrament, the Church offers a physical and visible symbol (water, oil, bread, wine, a man and woman in love, hands extended in absolution, and a man called to serve the Church), and through the transforming power of the Holy Spirit invoked every time, the symbol becomes the reality of Christ's saving, loving, and healing presence. Perhaps this dynamic is most profoundly visible in the case of the Eucharist, when the Church offers bread and wine that become the sacramental Body and Blood of Christ.

For Catholics, the Eucharist is of paramount importance, for it forms the Church, extends the Paschal Mystery of Jesus' death and Resurrection, proclaims the Word, and feeds us with the Body and Blood of Christ. In the Mass, we share already the life of Heaven. That's why when people ask me what I think Heaven will be like, I always reply that it will be a lot like going to Mass!

In Heaven, we will worship and praise God, we will be gathered in a perfect communion of love, mercy, peace, and truth, and we will be one around the table of the marriage feast of the Lamb. Those three actions and experiences are precisely the heart of what the Eucharist is about. We practice here on earth what we hope to do perfectly in the Kingdom of God.

When figures in Scripture experience the overwhelming awesomeness of God's presence, their immediately reflexive response is twofold: they intensely feel their littleness and unworthiness and they worship the Lord.

Worship of God is the most human of activities, known and practiced in every culture throughout history. The original meaning of "cult" is not some weird group that brainwashes people, but rather "a system of religious veneration and devotion"[4] that creates human community through a shared and practiced faith, which explains the deepest meaning of our common existence and experience.

"Cult", properly understood and lived, creates "culture", which constitutes a whole set of beliefs, assumptions, practices, and relationships that flow from a particular way of looking at the divine and the human. If the practice of "cult" becomes erratic or warped, "culture" will be thrown into a profound crisis. Much food for thought lies in such a truth.

If the communal worship of God and the celebration of the sacraments are at the very heart of our faith and our humanity, we should be troubled by the fact that on any given Sunday, prior to the COVID-19 pandemic, roughly 80 percent of our baptized Catholics are usually not celebrating the Eucharist. This downward trend is also reflected in the numbers of baptisms, confirmations, confessions, marriages, and priests. The lack of sacramental practice points to both a deep spiritual crisis in our culture and a profound need for formation, conversion, and dynamism among our leaders and people.

If we are doing the work of evangelization by spreading the Word and inviting people to Church, we need to make sure that we are asking them to become part of a community that is lively, flourishing, welcoming, and loving, a parish that celebrates the sacraments well where the preaching is excellent, both in its consolation and challenge, the music is uplifting and participatory, and the people are highly engaged. If Catholic faith and practice lead up to and flow from the Eucharist, then we organize everything around this sacred principle.

---

[4] Lexico.com, s.v. "cult" (Oxford University Press, 2020), https://www.lexico.com/en/definition/cult.

Our challenge is to celebrate the sacraments with greater understanding, zeal, love, and gratitude and to invite others to experience the grace of God in them as we have been touched, healed, forgiven, and loved through their efficacious power. The sacraments make the fullness of Jesus Christ present, who, in turn, makes the fullness of God present.

It is as simple and profound as that!

Only God Could Have Created
the Catholic Faith

Discipleship and formation is a key component of ecclesial life that expresses the essence of Jesus' Great Commission given right before He ascended to Heaven: "Go therefore and make disciples of all nations."[1]

As beloved children of God, baptized into the mystery of Christ and His Church, each of us is called to grow as a disciple of the Lord—rooted in prayer, nourished in the sacraments, immersed in the Scriptures, active in our faith community, serving the poor and marginalized, and in all of that, forming other disciples.

Disciples make other disciples. That's what we do because we cannot keep the Good News of Jesus Christ crucified and risen to ourselves.

As we know with anything, discipleship does not automatically happen. We can't just plop people in a church pew, give them the sacraments, have them do a service project or two, drop them off at religious education, and assume that they will develop a deep relationship with Christ and the Church. This formation into discipleship requires a fully engaged community: parents and families who practice their faith, high-quality religious formation experiences that form both the head and the heart, and teachers and catechists who are serious Christian disciples themselves.

[1] Mt 28:19.

In other words, we need to build a Catholic culture in which our young people naturally fall in love with God, develop a profound spiritual life, understand and articulate their faith, and take their rightful place in the Mystical Body of Christ.

The biggest challenge to forming young Catholics is forming their parents. It stands to reason that if a father and mother practice the faith themselves, participate in the sacraments and the parish, and build their marriage and family around Jesus Christ, their children have a far higher chance of embracing and living the faith themselves.

I applaud the many parents who heroically live their faith, seeking to pass it on to their children and sacrificing much to give them a solid Catholic upbringing. They are the generous hearts who keep the Church alive.

We also know that some parents send their children to Catholic schools and religious education programs, but do not go to Mass themselves, know little about the faith, and never speak of God at home. Too often our children get the mixed message that Church and faith are supposedly important, but in the actuality of daily life, not as significant as sports, leisure time, sleeping in on Sundays, or just about anything else. We need to reach creatively and effectively those parents who are not yet engaged.

Another consistent need for the Church is the formation of Catholic school teachers and catechists. If we seek to form our young people as Christian disciples, fully alive in the Lord, then those who are privileged to serve as their Catholic faith mentors must be disciples themselves. I am deeply grateful for the remarkable servants who generously serve in our schools and formation programs, teaching about the love and mystery of God, the centrality of Christ and the goodness, and the truth and beauty of our faith. Theirs is a noble and challenging task!

Through ongoing study, prayer, and formation, our teachers and catechists need to grow in their own discipleship if they hope to pass the faith onto their students. A Catholic mentor who does not faithfully participate in the Eucharist, Reconciliation, daily prayer, and the general life of the Church will only be a weak trumpet.

Before the Second Vatican Council, most young Catholics memorized the *Baltimore Catechism* and were able to give back answers to basic questions about the faith. There was little emphasis given to spirituality, prayer, and the need to develop a loving relationship with Jesus Christ. Formation was very much about the head rather than the heart.

In the years after the council, the pendulum swung the other way. Content became less important than experience. I remember making a lot of collages and banners in grade school. The focus was much more on love than it was on truth. Today, we are trying to strike the right balance, knowing that faith formation impacts all aspects of our lives, that we need both content and context, that a living and loving relationship with God is key, but we also want our young people to know the basics of their faith. We want more knowledge of the Scriptures and the saints. We want to help our youth to experience God and act out in their experience the life of the Gospel.

These reflections all lead to a very central point: the importance of adult formation. Our young people will catch the faith if they see us adults fully engaged and alive in the beauty of the Church, if we are serious about our discipleship, and if Mass, prayer, and service in the community are truly at the center of our lives.

When I was a parish priest, I was always passionate about adult formation, offering series on the Scriptures, prayer, the sacraments, the saints, social teaching, and

Church history. Our Catholic faith is so rich and deep, so true and beautiful, that only God could have created it all! We will never grasp it all in our lifetime, but what a joyous adventure to drink in as much as we can.

The Sacred Door of Holy Baptism

We close the Christmas season with the celebration of the Baptism of the Lord. The Church invites us, through this feast, to ponder the truth, beauty, and goodness of our own baptisms in Christ, when we became adopted children of the Father, put on the Lord Jesus, were washed clean of Original Sin, were filled with sanctifying grace, and became members of the Church.

As Saint Paul declares many times in his epistles, Baptism is the sacred door through which we enter into the fullness of relationship with God.[1] Who Jesus is by nature—that is, the beloved Son of the Father—we become through the regenerating waters of Baptism: beloved children of God. This divine sonship or daughtership has become our deepest identity. Just as Jesus heard the voice of the Father declaring, "This is my beloved Son," at His Baptism,[2] so God lovingly whispered the same words at ours. How different our world would be if every Christian recognized themselves and others as children of God.

In Baptism, we put on the Lord Jesus and enter into His priesthood. Symbolized by the white gown, this call to live Jesus is the basis and purpose of all vocations within the Church. The ministerial priesthood of deacons, priests, and bishops only exists in order to serve the baptized priesthood of the laity. Called to make the world holy, lay faithful rub

---

[1] See Rom 6:3–11; Gal 3:26–27; Col 2:11–13; cf. Tit 3:5.
[2] Mt 3:17; cf. Mk 1:11; Lk 3:22.

shoulders with all sorts of people who will never come and talk to a priest (or a bishop, for that matter!). You may be the only Christ a neighbor, relative, friend, or co-worker will ever meet. Your words of faith may be the only creed another ever hears. Your deeds of compassion may be the only love someone ever experiences. How important our witness to Christ becomes when we look at it in that vast panorama of salvation.

Because of Original Sin, there is an inherent selfishness in human nature and we are born into a world that has been warped and misshaped by countless generations of sinful actions. Baptism saves us from all of that and claims us for the Kingdom of Heaven. Like a front-end alignment on a truck, this first sacrament reorders our fundamental being toward God, grace, and goodness, so we can zoom down the highway of salvation and righteousness. Because we are still saints in the making, the Church gives us the Sacrament of Reconciliation, so that when we do sin, we can recapture our baptismal innocence and start our moral life afresh.

Those old enough to remember the *Baltimore Catechism* know that sanctifying grace is the indwelling of the Holy Trinity in our very being. As Jesus says in the Gospel of John, those who love Him and keep His Commandments will experience the very life of God living within them. "We will come to him and make our home with him."[3]

Beginning in Baptism, God comes to live within us in a particular way. God is no longer simply above us or outside of us, but now deeply within our very being. Every sacrament received increases this mysterious divine life within us; only sin pushes God away. Just ponder the amazing truth that God, whom the entire universe cannot contain,

[3] Jn 14:23.

wants to live, breathe, and act in you; that is how much He loves you and takes delight in your being!

Baptism makes us members of the Church, part of the Mystical Body of Christ, united to both saints in Heaven and fellow pilgrims on earth. Without the Church, we would be lost and alone; we would not know God or ourselves without her; she nourishes our souls with the Word, feeds us with the Body and Blood of Christ, proclaims the forgiveness of Christ, and leads us to eternal life. As baptized Christians, the Church is the mystery we live for and attempt to serve; she is the only institution that I would readily die for. All of the blessings and graces we receive as Catholics flood our lives through the sacred door of Holy Baptism.

So rejoice today in the gift and mystery of your human, baptized, miraculous, and holy life! God created you, gave you a soul and a name, entrusted you with a vocation and a purpose, and wants you to live with Him forever. If you don't already know this, research the place and date of your Baptism. Celebrate your anniversary of new life in Christ!

The Cross of Marriage

The Catholic Church has always been articulate and passionate about marriage and family, because we experience the sacred love of God in these relationships in a definitive and profound way. From the beginning of creation, God willed man and woman to find fulfillment in each other and to be faithful and fruitful, loving each other in the full freedom of their Heavenly Father. Although Original Sin broke the integrity of this holy marriage, God never gave up on us. Instead, He sent His Son to heal, redeem, and forgive what was wounded and broken in us.

As Christians, we view Jesus as the Divine Bridegroom who came in search of His Bride, the One who turns the plain water of our unredeemed nature into the rich wine of sacred union with God. In wedding homilies, I always liken Jesus' Cross to a marriage bed, for it is in the Crucifixion that Jesus lays Himself down body, soul, mind, and heart and completely hands His life over for the sake of His Bride, the Church, which Jesus both brings to life and marries through His death and Resurrection.

That means that marriage is a little bit like crucifixion. In marriage, something has to surrender and die so that something greater can come to life. Both husband and wife are called to let go of their individual, self-directed, autonomous lives so that this beautiful new communion of two lives entwined with each other and wrapped around Christ can come to life. Marriage will never succeed unless both spouses put Christ and the well-being and needs of each other before their own. True love is nourished by sacrifice—a love that gives itself away, a love that lays down its life for the sake of the other. When both spouses heroically strive to live this crucified and risen love of Christ in their marriage, they unleash the creative and saving power of God, even to the point of co-creating with God brand new human beings. Marital fidelity will always be fruitful.

Pope John Paul II boldly stated that a Christian family living the love of God in a communion of faith, service, support, and sacrifice becomes a joyful icon or window into the inner life of the Trinity.[1] Jesus reveals the very life of God as relationship—the Father loving and begetting the Son, the Son returning that divine gift in radical surrender, and the Holy Spirit generated as Love. So too, a married couple who give themselves to each other—body, soul, mind, and heart—in the sacramental union of grace incarnate the marriage between Christ and the Church; they shine forth in their children a holy relationship of persons, where each one becomes more fully himself or herself in the context of family.

The Church seeks to reach out with compassion, support, and accompaniment to all of our brothers and sisters who experience the sadness of marital separation and divorce, those who have a same-sex orientation, those who live together in nonmarital unions, and those who simply reject the Church's sexual and life teachings. We need to be patient, loving, and inviting toward everyone who finds himself in these challenging situations and often complex relationships. We also need to be prophetic because our Catholic teaching on the dignity of the human person, the

---

[1] See Pope John Paul II, Letter to Families *Gratissimam Sane* (February 2, 1994), par. 6, http://www.vatican.va/content/john-paul-ii/en/letters/1994/documents/hf_jp-ii_let_02021994_families.html.

glory of our sexuality, the spiritual meaning of marriage, and the absolute importance of family are gifts of divine revelation that help us build a civilization of life, love, justice, joy, and mercy.

Sadly, our culture today has lost sight of God's loving plan for our sexuality, marriage, and family life. The sexual revolution, the contraceptive mentality, and the legalization of abortion have led many people to see the sacred gift of sexual relations as sensual gratification, marriage as a conditional and temporary living arrangement, and family as any group of people that we choose to define as such. The best way that we can give witness to the joy of the Gospel and the saving power of Jesus Christ is to strive to live an integrated, pure, and selfless life—for those who are married to make their sacrament extraordinary in its concern for the other, and for families to spend more time praying, playing, and enjoying each other. We give thanks to God for our parents, our families, our spouses, our siblings, our children, and our friendships. Even in our challenges and trials, God has given us each other as a sacred gift! What a grace. What a responsibility.

The Gift of Family Life

Marriage and family are significant components of the Church's mission. As evidenced by Pope Francis' 2016 post-synodal apostolic exhortation *Amoris Laetitia*, the Catholic Church wants to serve, form, support, and help married couples and families to live their essential vocation with faith, hope, love, joy, and generosity.

Our theology and spirituality of marriage and family life is so rich, deep, and beautiful because we see these sacred covenants as sacraments of God's inner Trinitarian life and the spousal relationship between Christ and the Church. Marriage and family lived well manifest how God loves and relates to us.

Yet we all know how challenging marriage and family life can be. Women and men think and communicate very differently. Busy schedules today allow little time to nurture familial relationships. Many couples choose to live together without a permanent commitment. Work, parenting, schedules, crises, and conflicts can overwhelm. And many marriages end in separation or divorce.

The Church wants to draw close to married couples and families to support them in living out their vocation, to offer welcome and healing to those who experience the pain of familial breakdown, and to prepare couples well who are engaged to be married.

The Church sees the family as the domestic church because it is within the sacred and unique bonds of parents and children that we first experience God's love and nurture, learn how to pray, and come to believe. If the Church is an outward expression of God's inner life of self-giving and loving—in other words, if the Church is a family—then every individual family lives that same mystery.

In praying and struggling, in fighting and forgiving, in working and playing, in loving and sacrificing, and ultimately, in joining together with the parish family to celebrate the Eucharist, each family incarnates the very life and grace of God.

I have great memories of my childhood when growing up with five brothers in a small house, learning to share toys, chores, limited space, and parental attention. We prayed the Rosary every night after supper, whether we wanted to or not. We went to early Mass every Sunday and sometimes during the week. My parents were deeply involved in our lives, yet gave us freedom in appropriate ways.

I learned that life was not essentially about me, that things went better when we worked together, that sometimes we each need to sacrifice ourselves for the good of the others, and that I would not always get my way. I also came to experience the presence and love of God within my family and the world. I learned how to love, believe, and work for the common good.

So how can the Church be a better support to families, especially those who are hurting and broken? How do we not only more effectively prepare engaged couples for the life and beauty ahead of them, but also be there three, five, or even ten years later?

How do we offer effective support to persons and families who are going through the pain of separation and divorce? How do we better catechize and form young people in the beauty and truth of their own sexuality as a divine gift meant for marital intimacy and the creation of children? And that we are sexually wired to give love and life to others?

How do we walk with those who may experience confusion about their sexual identity or are suffering the effects of abuse? How do we welcome and serve Catholics with same-sex attractions with sincerity and love? How do we teach couples, families, and children to pray together and individually? How do we fuse love and truth as well as the teachings of the Church and pastoral application to concrete situations?

In *Amoris Laetitia*, Pope Francis reminds us that family life is not a problem to be solved but rather a gift to be embraced and a vocation to incarnate God's love and grace in the world. We should never diminish or water down the high ideals of marriage and family that Catholicism presents, but we need to translate that beautiful theology and spirituality in language, programs, and action that truly help married couples, parents, and children to understand the spiritual meaning of their lives, bound together in Christ as a domestic church—a sacred circle of love, grace, mercy, prayer, faith, and service.

The Faith of the Young

Whenever I am blessed to interact with young Catholics, I am always inspired by beautiful examples of faith, challenged with searching questions, admiring of a deep desire for God and authenticity, and praying for their spiritual growth and protection in this world of such enormous possibilities and potential dangers.

One January, Kevin Driscoll, the director of the Youth and Young Adult ministry in Gary, Indiana, offered a twenty-four-hour retreat for young Catholics, which I was privileged to be a part of. Eighty young people responded! I was amazed and edified; the experience taught me that our young people are thirsty for God, idealistic about changing the world, and wanting to make their unique contribution to the Church. Sometimes, we oldsters can dismissively discount the insights and gifts of young people, unconsciously shutting them out of full participation in the life of our communities.

What a tragedy that is! Whenever I ask anybody what concerns him the most about the Church, the response invariably is, "We need to reach our young people and keep them active in the faith."

Several years ago, I read a remarkable book entitled *Young Catholic America: Emerging Adults In, Out of, and Gone from the Church*. Authored by a group of sociologists who tracked a study group of eighteen-year-old active Catholics for seven years, the book offers some conclusions about what factors seem to determine which young

Catholics stay active in the Church in their twenties and which simply check out.

The determinants were the following: Catholics who learned the basics of the faith, read Scripture, discovered a method of prayer, had parents or an adult figure who modeled faith for them, and found a community that supported their discipleship had far better odds of remaining active in the Church. The role of fathers who modeled faith and were engaged in their children's lives was highly significant.

These conclusions give us direction concerning where we need to put our efforts regarding young Catholics. The impact of parents and adult figures as role models of active Catholic discipleship is huge.

How do we help form parents themselves in the faith, so that they, in turn, will form their children? I point to my parents' example of belief, prayer, and involvement in the Church as the single most significant inspiration for my vocation to the priesthood. How do we teach our young people how to read, study, and pray the Scriptures so that the narrative of salvation in the Bible makes sense to them as the interpretive key for their own lives?

We talk about prayer all the time, but do we really teach people how to pray, developing a method and discipline that works for them? Continuing to study the basic teachings of the Church, serve the poor and marginalized, and become active in a parish that nurtures discipleship must be priority goals for all of us in leading, forming, serving, and loving young Catholics. Clearly, we need to embrace our own faith with generosity and conviction if we hope to create a spiritual culture that will nurture and develop the religious sensibilities of the young.

I want our young people to be engaged in the synod process all the way through, from the parish sessions through the deanery meetings, to the synod itself and beyond. Their voices and experiences need to be heard because they not only live the faith now, but will carry it forward well into this twenty-first century, decades after us older folk are gone.

Also, don't forget about our high school students, collegians, and emerging adults. They want to live their faith, find a nurturing community, embrace high ideals, change the world, and live authentically. When we think of the Scriptures, many of the most prominent individuals were young—for example, King David, Jeremiah, the Virgin Mary, and many of the Apostles. When we ponder the saints, many of them reached the heights of spiritual perfection at a very young age—for example, Thérèse of Lisieux, Aloysius Gonzaga, John Berchmans, Tarcisius, and Maria Goretti.

I want to affirm my great love, esteem, and admiration for young people. In all of the events and encounters I have had with them, I am always inspired, amazed, encouraged, and fired up.

I ask our young people to not give up on the Church or on adults. Things may move too slowly sometimes; maybe we don't always listen or welcome each other. Regardless, this is your moment to know and live Jesus, to build the Kingdom of God, and to allow the fresh breath of the Holy Spirit to breathe on us anew.

I count on you to help us become fully ourselves in Christ. I love you!

Children of God

One of the astonishing truths of our faith that can keep us grounded and joyful through the hardest times is our divine filiation or spiritual adoption in Jesus Christ. Let me explain.

As Christians, we believe that in Jesus Christ—His life, death, and Resurrection—we receive a new identity, initiated at Baptism, by which we enter into the very life of the Blessed Trinity as sons and daughters of the Father. The Sonship that Jesus enjoys in relation to the Father and Holy Spirit is graciously shared with us.

In multiple places in his epistles, Saint Paul articulates his understanding of spiritual adoption.[1] On a mystical level, Paul came to believe that the Christ event fundamentally changed humanity's relationship to God. Jesus gains for us the forgiveness of sins, the promise of eternal salvation, and a new intimacy with God, sprung from our filial relationship with the Father.

Jesus loves us so much that He shares His total self, even His divine relationships. Clinging to nothing as His own, Jesus opens up His own relation to the Father to us. What He is by nature, we become through divine adoption. In Baptism, we can call God "Abba" just as Jesus does, because we are sons and daughters of the Father, brothers and sisters of Jesus, and temples of the Holy Spirit. One gets the sense in Paul's writings that he never got over the amazing graciousness of this divine filiation.

[1] For example, see Romans 8, Galatians 4, and Ephesians 1.

As Paul says, we are children of God, baptized into the priesthood of Jesus Christ, anointed by the Holy Spirit, created for love, and destined to live forever. When we fall into sin or despair, we suffer from temporary amnesia; we have forgotten who we are.

I know this probably sounds crazy, but when I am walking through an airport or sitting on a subway, I feel the urge to go up to people and ask them if they know they are children of God. Maybe they do, but oftentimes it seems we have lost our way, as we painfully see the violence, poverty, hatred, and disregard for human life that daily wracks our planet.

When we know our identity in Christ and our divine purpose, we can do all things through the One who strengthens us.[2] Our lives matter, and what we do in this life has eternal implications.

All of us struggle to love ourselves authentically. I know people who almost despise themselves, so often because they were not loved and nurtured as children. When we wholeheartedly embrace our identity as children of God, we can ground our self-esteem in the love of the Father. Then it doesn't matter so much what other people think of us, or even what we think of ourselves.

The greatest truth is that God finds us loveable and good. I find the greatest antidote to self-hatred, despair, fear, anger, and self-pity to be a solid meditation on spiritual adoption.

When the saints experienced the extraordinary love of God, they came to know themselves—the deep and real "soul" of their human nature, as a daughter or son of the Father, loved and created to love. When Paul experienced Jesus on the road to Damascus, when Francis of Assisi

---

[2] See Phil 4:13.

kissed a leper, when Augustine heard Ambrose preaching, when Thérèse of Lisieux read 1 Corinthians, when Edith Stein observed a stranger at prayer, when Mother Teresa picked up her first dying person, an explosion of divine love occurred that changed them forever.

The extraordinary deeds of the saints are grounded in their self-understanding as children of God.

Try meditating every day for several minutes on who you are in Jesus Christ. Go to the index of the *Catechism of the Catholic Church* and look up the passages on adoption in Christ. When I do this, I find peace, patience with others and myself, a deeper ability to forgive, and a greater capacity to see the bigger picture; I find it easier to love others because they are children of God as well.

In Heaven, we will all be walking around more radiant than the sun, filled with the glory of God and free of sin, conflict, and division. So why do we need to wait until then to live out our identity as beloved children of the Father? Let's go live it now!

The Gospel of Life

I recently saw the following quote on Facebook: "The source of all our social problems today is the idea that some people's lives are less valuable than others." I could not agree more.

The Church invites us to ponder the dignity of the human person, created in the image and likeness of God and redeemed by Jesus Christ. The fundamental cornerstone of Catholic moral teaching is the infinite value of all human life, from conception to natural death, with no exceptions or exclusions.

A cursory glance at a newspaper, or a simple view of the nightly news, painfully reveals how far away this ideal remains and how we seem to be moving even more in the wrong direction. Terrorism, mass shootings, and deadly and daily violence in our streets consistently grab the headlines; but our society continues also to accept and perpetuate abortion, euthanasia, capital punishment, poverty, abuse, and neglect, issues that get less press but remain constant. These attacks on human life and dignity are so commonplace and widespread that they oftentimes fail to capture our attention or disturb our conscience.

Gaudium et Spes, Vatican II's 1965 Pastoral Constitution on the Church in the Modern World, calls abortion "an abominable crime",[1] but it sadly continues to be legal in

---

[1] *Gaudium et Spes*, no. 51, in *Vatican Council II: The Conciliar and Postconciliar Documents*, new rev. ed., ed. Austin Flannery, O.P. (Collegeville, Minn.: Liturgical Press, 2014).

our country. How can a society predicated on the ringing words "We hold these truths to be self-evident, that all people have the right to life, liberty, and the pursuit of happiness" continue to allow and approve the destruction of human life in the womb?

How many more millions of unborn children must die before we come to our moral senses? I am grateful that our parishes and Catholic Charities offer so much concrete assistance to women who face crisis pregnancies. We must not only denounce the destructive evil of abortion, but we must also create a culture of life where mothers and fathers can easily accept the gift of a child because they are surrounded by love, support, and resources. We strive to bring healing and hope to everyone who has been wounded by abortion.

I recently celebrated the funerals of two suicide victims, both young people in their twenties with everything to live for. Suicide rates are increasing among certain sectors of our community. How can we be more supportive of those who struggle with depression, mental illness, or grave crises in their lives?

How can we reach the young with Jesus' message of hope, love, and purpose? How profoundly sad to think that many young people feel such hopelessness that they see no way out except death and they think they have no one to talk to about it. Through Catholic Charities we can offer a support group for those who mourn a loved one who took his own life.

Euthanasia and physician-assisted suicide are gaining greater traction in our society. Even in all of its pain, if suffering has no inherent meaning in life and is not seen fundamentally as a gift, then ending a life of pain and difficulty makes sense on some level. As people of faith, however, we need to lift up the dignity and worth of the sick and the disabled, helping others to see that the weak and suffering in our midst offer a great treasure of love, wisdom, and perseverance. Do we really want a culture that eliminates lives that are no longer seen as productive or valuable?

Many states continue to embrace capital punishment. Many of the people on death row have committed heinous crimes, but they are still children of God and worthy of life, love, and forgiveness. Because they are a threat to society, many may need to be incarcerated their whole lives, but can they still make some sort of contribution to the common good through work, conversion, and prayer?

Because God never gives up on anyone, neither can we. I will never forget my visit to death row in Michigan City, Indiana; it was a moving experience of faith, prayer, and the power of contrition.

All of the recent popes have powerfully called Catholics to build a culture of life and a civilization of love, where every human person is welcomed, respected, and loved, where everybody receives what they need to live a dignified existence as a child of God and can also make their own contribution to the common good.

The Church will never stop proclaiming the Gospel of life and working toward this realization until every child has the right to be born; children living in poverty, abuse, or neglect are loved; the ill, disabled, and dying are supported and affirmed; the hungry are fed; the young have hope; victims of violent crime find healing; and prisoners are acknowledged as children of the Father. The poverty, injustice, hunger, and violence of this world are powerful, destructive, and overwhelming, but love is stronger and far-reaching.

May each of our lives help heal this broken world that God holds so close and has already redeemed.

Secrets and Lessons of Autumn

October is my favorite month! The crisp mornings, the radiant color of the falling leaves, the sunny days, and harvest moons all make me happy to live in the Midwest. When I lived in the tropics, autumn was the season I missed the most. Nature puts on her finest dress before surrendering to the winter snows and chilling cold. I find a sweet melancholy in these autumn days, pondering the glory of the faded summer and anticipating the wintery season of cold and darkness.

We all experience moments and seasons of disturbing disorientation—the sudden loss of a job, a heartbreaking divorce, the tragic death of someone close to us, an unexpected illness, or the increasing difficulties of old age. We all want to hang on to the familiar, the reassuring, and the security of life as we know it to be and are comfortable with. Like Simon Peter on Mount Tabor,[1] we want to build permanent booths at our present existential site and just hunker down in the satisfying routine that grounds us. We want to hang on to the summer of life and never see it end.

Autumn has secrets and lessons to teach us about surrender, acceptance, and humility in the face of the many changes and challenges of our lives—as we observe a beautifully bold oak tree through the seasons, its leaves gradually turn color as the green energy of summer fades away,

[1] Mt 17:1–8; Mk 9:2–8; and Lk 9:28–36.

and one by one, the leaves fall to the ground in a dizzying swirl of surrender and finality. By the end of November, the tree is a maze of stripped black branches, silhouetted against the gray sky, bracing itself for the onslaught of winter but silently and gracefully standing tall as always.

Nature imitates the Paschal Mystery as Christ moves through the seasons of His own life, ministering, forgiving, healing, and preaching to the people in the high summer of His mighty divine power.

And then autumn hits!

The crowds melt away; the disciples desert Jesus. His earthly ministry ends, and He is left alone to face the terror of His Passion—stripped of His clothes, insulted, beaten, and tortured, embracing the Cross as it is lifted high in the morning air, left to die as a common criminal. Jesus never looked less powerful or consequential than He did on the Cross. Yet, in that winter of death, He accomplished the mighty deed of our salvation by surrendering to the seeming destruction of all that He had come to know, love, and do. Whenever I see a bare tree, stripped of its leaves and life, I think of the Cross.

So much of our anger, frustration, fear, anxiety, and dread flow from our inability to surrender to the unknown, the unknown of new health limitations, the loss of a friend, the end of a familiar life's chapter, the inevitability of death. Grieving well is so important because it allows us to cry over our loss, name our fears and sadness, mourn who and what has departed from our vision, and hopefully move on with greater wisdom, gratitude, love, and acceptance.

People who get stuck in the grieving process cannot let go of their loss and can easily be enveloped in a sad web of depression, anger, and hopelessness. When we have faced our own dark nights, wept over our losses without shame, and surrendered to the challenge of new situations, God can powerfully use us to heal and help others.

Both of my parents, whom I love deeply, have been dead for a number of years now. I have driven past the house where we all lived for many years and longed to be able to drive up, open the door, and find them there with supper on the table and an abundance of smiles and hugs to go around. But I will never again experience that unique joy of being with them in this life. I feel sad, grateful, and ultimately hopeful when I ponder the stubborn, unchangeable fact of their death and lingering physical absence.

Thankful for what has been, sad that it will never be again in this life, yet hopeful for the ultimate and eternal rest in the Kingdom of God, I choose to move forward, feeling the strength of faith and love that my parents imparted to me for all those years.

How sweet life becomes when we can ultimately come to see every loss, hurt, change, and death as a beautiful and necessary part of God's plan for us, when we can move through the seasons of life with determination, freedom, acceptance, and grace.

The people who have experienced unspeakable suffering, heartbreaking losses, and terrible tragedies and have come out on the other side—wounded but victorious, changed but not broken—are examples and models for us.

In their desert sojourn to the Promised Land, some of the Israelites wanted to return to Egypt, to the difficult but comforting slavery they had known, a servitude that was less scary than this vast freedom under the desert sky.

Whenever I want to go back to Egypt, I ponder a tree in the October sun, praying for the bravery needed to kiss the Cross.

Hand Our Lives over to God

When I participated in my first biannual Priests' Convocation, a four-day gathering of our priests to reflect on a particular topic, pray, socialize, and relax together, I was looking forward to it with great expectations.

Terry Sullivan, who works for Guest House, a treatment center for priests who suffer addictions, spoke to us about embracing a healthy lifestyle.

Not surprisingly, Terry devoted much of his talks to addictions and the twelve-step process of Alcoholics Anonymous, which has helped millions to overcome their addictions and go on to live balanced and happy lives.

When you think about it, all of us are addicted to something, tempted to fill the holes in our lives with alcohol, drugs, money, material things, overwork, television, computer time, or food. Only when we awaken to our powerlessness over particular situations—things and relationships in our lives that have become unhealthy—can we begin to move toward surrender and freedom.

In chapter 12 of his Second Letter to the Corinthians, Saint Paul admits that some "thorn in the flesh" plagued and defeated him. After praying for it to go away (whatever it was, Paul doesn't say), he surrenders it to the Lord, acknowledging his weakness and total dependence on God.

Paradoxically, Paul finds liberation in this admission of failure, for God's power is made manifest in human weakness. In the apostle's experience lies a great lesson for us. How often do we try to force a change of behavior in someone else, or even within ourselves, to no avail?

We try to effect transformation with a hammer of will and determination, only to end in defeat and anger. Only when we admit our powerlessness and lack of control can the grace of God work precisely in our acknowledged weakness. We cannot change anyone except ourselves, and then only with gentleness and surrender.

In handing our lives over to the Lord, we humbly profess that God is God and we are not. Easier said than done!

How often in prayer are we really asking God to do our will, to see things our way, rather than, like Jesus in the Garden of Gethsemane, handing our will and heart over to the Father? Our need to control, to possess, and to bend other people to our point of view and opinions about everything is so strongly rooted in us that we are almost unaware of it.

When we don't get our way, which is almost a constant occurrence, we turn toward a quick fix to blur our anger, fear, and depression, so that we can still feel in control and powerful. While feeding addictions initially gives us those good feelings we crave, the tables are soon reversed and we find ourselves serving alcohol, food, money, or whatever we turn to in our emptiness besides God.

The whole process of conversion outlined by Jesus in the Gospels is a path of surrender, humility, and prayer, whereby we allow God to dethrone the imperious demands of the false self, that inner voice that is constantly judging, planning, complaining, criticizing, and controlling, that part of us that is usually angry and fearful. When we hand our lives over to God and stop thinking we are the center of the universe, life gets a whole lot better—more joyful, peaceful, loving, and deep. The saints acted out this path of spiritual liberation, whereby they were set free to do the works of the Kingdom.

At the convocation, Terry told us that a good sign that someone is on the road to recovery is the presence of gratitude. When we are angry, fearful, and filled with resentment, little room exists for love and thanksgiving. Being authentically grateful manifests an inner liberation whereby we can truly see the wonders and blessings of our lives with the clear vision of grace.

Until we can let go of the wounds and hurts of the past, break away from toxic relationships and substances, surrender the poison of shame, regret, and anger, and be able to forgive both ourselves and others, we will not be fully free to become the people that God has called us to be. Until we have somehow embraced our true selves, we will not be able to give ourselves away in service, sacrifice, and love.

As you can see, the convocation was fruitful! I am grateful for the time spent with our priests. They are good men who have given their lives to the service of Christ and the Church. Many of them are overworked and tired. Nevertheless, they tirelessly proclaim the Gospel to us, celebrate the sacraments of God's grace, and pastor us through the joys, challenges, and sorrows of this life. Theirs is not an easy task, but they embrace and live it with sacrifice and goodness.

Maybe we could all take a moment to write a note to our priests, telling them of our love and gratitude.

Living the Year of Mercy

Sunday, November 20, 2016, the Feast of Christ the King, marked the closing of the Jubilee Year of Mercy. This blessed time was a grace for Catholics around the world, as we focused on the mercy of God poured out through Jesus Christ as the means of our salvation and reconciliation.

The Jubilee Year inspired many people to celebrate the Sacrament of Reconciliation with greater frequency, depth, preparation, appreciation, and gratitude. In confessing our sins, we come to realize our radical need for a Savior for mercy and forgiveness, for peace and healing in the world. I personally have come to appreciate this sacrament more during the Year of Mercy, both as a sinner and as a confessor.

The Year of Mercy moved many people to live out the corporal and spiritual works of mercy with fervor, generosity, and joy.

Many Catholics went on pilgrimages to experience the special grace of this Jubilee. In October 2016, I accompanied two groups to Rome and Assisi, as well as accompanying the World Youth Day pilgrims to Poland in July. In Rome, we visited all four major basilicas, entering the Holy Doors in each as we prayed and meditated on the mercy and love of God. Journeys to sacred places change us, as we experience the breadth and depth of our Catholic faith in very tangible ways, coming to know the lives of the saints and the power of prayer in new ways.

I would hope that we were all inspired to reconcile conflicts, forgive past hurts, break down old walls, reach out to someone who needs love and attention, and make the mercy of God real in all of our relationships. Maybe our efforts were not all well received, maybe some people are not yet ready to move on or let go, but the Good News of the Gospel tells us that we can and should extend mercy. As I get older, I realize more and more that life is just way too short and precious to even waste a minute being angry about little things that people say and do or being upset about what we can do nothing about. When we truly forgive, the first people set free are ourselves.

How do we keep up the good practices we embraced in the Jubilee Year? How do we keep this time of grace alive and fresh in our spiritual practice, so that the changes we have effected will continue to flourish?

We do this by continuing to do what we have done—by making scriptural reflection; receiving the sacraments of the Eucharist and Reconciliation regularly in our lives; striving to be peacemakers in all of our relationships and conversations; practicing the works of mercy in new and exciting ways; and unconditionally loving the other, regardless of the response. This will keep our faith from ever being routine and the Year of Mercy from being a pleasant but distant memory.

Mercy is what love practices when it comes up against suffering and misery. In this context, we can view the whole Christ event as a rescue mission of mercy. God comes in search of us, to seek and save what was lost, as Jesus says to Zacchaeus. How significant are Luke's Gospel stories of the Parable of the Prodigal Son; the Good Shepherd; Zacchaeus; the lost coin; the narrative of the sinful woman who anointed Jesus' feet at the house of Simon the Pharisee; and the Parable of the Pharisee and the Publican.

All of these Gospel messages reinforce the central message of mercy: God loves us so much that He could not bear to watch us suffer the anguish of sin and death alone, so He sent His Son to us in human form to search us out wherever we have been hiding, to heal everything that is lost, broken, and dead within us and to lead us as sons and daughters of the Father into the Kingdom of God.

I praise God for all of the grace, forgiveness, love, solidarity, service, and joy that we experienced in the Jubilee Year of Mercy! May it only continue to grow and flourish.

Praise God for His infinite and tender mercy!

The Mysticism of Gratitude

The greatest mystics and saints in our Church show us the path of holiness—a movement of surrender to the love and will of yearning for prayer and things of the Spirit, and a greater vision of truth, beauty, and goodness. People like Teresa of Avila, Thomas Merton, Dorothy Day, John of the Cross, and Mother Teresa prove that the closer you get to God, the simpler life becomes. The complexities, distractions, and competing values of living in this world gently simmer away, like a gourmet reduction recipe. The radical and basic essence of reality remains.

The simplest things in life move and amaze the mystics and saints. Watching a sunrise, walking in the woods, talking with a homeless person on the street, sharing a meal with a friend, praying in a quiet chapel, playing with grandchildren, listening to the silence of nature, or observing the heavens on a clear night all become encounters with God. Such moments lead us to contemplation, where we simply are wrapped in the full reality of the present and understand in a deeply intuitive way the sacredness and unity of everything.

In a society that is increasingly distracted, virtual, and disconnected, our spirits profoundly hunger for simple experiences of God, others, nature, and our deepest selves.

Whenever I feel overwhelmed, sad, angry, or at loose ends, a walk in the dunes, a meal with a friend, deep prayer time in front of the Eucharist, or an hour with a good book bring sanity, healing, and connection back with great spiritual force. Without consistent moments of silence, contemplation, friendship, and peace, we start losing our humanity! If we never commune with the world that God made and are only immersed in artificial things, if we never look up, we will always think that we are the highest point.

Gratitude and thankfulness are hallmarks of the mystical journey. The more we discover the mystery, wonder, and miraculous nature of our human existence, the more grateful we become. Life is a gift handed to us on a silver platter by God, and even though pain, grief, and struggle may mark our days and wound our hearts, it is so great just to be!

Philosophically, we can say that our very lives are both a participation in and an extension of the life of God. The human race and the world could have easily gone on without us ever having been, but God thought otherwise, and we are grateful for the gift.

Often, when I preach on Thanksgiving Day, I fill a plastic laundry basket with things that I am grateful for, then bring it to Mass and use the homily to explain what the basket contains and why. Pictures of family and friends, books, my college diploma, the Bible, a crucifix, food, a prayer book, clothing, cross-country skis, tennis shoes, a health insurance card, and a myriad of other objects remind me that I am blessed beyond anything I could dare to ask for or imagine.

When I ponder the complex grace of my being— body, soul, mind, and heart—that I am made in the image and likeness of God, that the Lord seeks to dwell in me and love me forever, I am overwhelmed. When I meditate on Jesus and the Church; the power of the sacraments and the truth of the Scriptures; the forgiveness, kindness, and mercy that have always enveloped me, my heart sings a Magnificat of praise. When I think of family and friends, teachers and mentors, parishioners and strangers, who have accepted and loved me, supported and forgave me, gifted and carried me, it seems too good to be true. I am grateful for food and shelter, travel and books, education and health, freedom and purpose, trees and flowers, history and philosophy, vision and hearing, as well as the ability to walk, laugh, run, and climb.

I thank the Lord for calling me to serve the Church as a priest and now as a bishop. All of it is so mysterious, beautiful, strange, wonderful, and good. Life is so great, painful, funny, sad, hard, and joyful that it all has to mean something and be moving into something glorious.

What are you grateful for? What items would you place in the laundry basket and lift up to the Lord in a hymn of praise and thanks? Ingratitude, entitlement, and resentment will always seek a higher place and never be satisfied, while thankfulness happily takes the lowest place because it realizes how much has already been given.

The mystics show us that life is simple, pure, and good. The saints teach us that we are well on our way to the Kingdom of God when joy, praise, gratefulness, and generosity serve as the hallmark of our lives.

Let your life be more about praising than complaining, more about what has been given than what is lacking. Gratitude and humility contain the great secret of joy and peace. It's all so simple. What we are searching for has already been given. We just need to reach out and receive it and then pass it on.

The Glory of God

Scripture readings mention the glory of God in both the prophecy of Isaiah and Paul's Letter to the Romans.[1] The word "glory" is all over the Bible, the prayers of Mass, and the Liturgy of the Hours. Biblical figures glorify the Lord; the glory of God fills the Temple in the vision of Isaiah; we sing the Gloria at Mass; we pray to experience the glory of Heaven.

What exactly is glory?

Shekinah, a Hebrew word meaning both "glory" and "the divine presence", appears throughout the Old Testament whenever God shows the wonder of His revelation, whether in dialogue with Moses, dwelling in the Ark of the Covenant, appearing to the prophet Ezekiel, or leading the Israelites through the desert to the Promised Land.

When people experience the glory of God, they are overwhelmed, fearful, trembling, and often fall to the ground in awe. In the Jewish view, no one can see God directly and live, but the Lord would reveal His glory, His *shekinah*, as a way for them to come close.

Another Hebrew word that speaks of divine glory is *kavod*, closely related to *kaved*, which means "heavy" or "weightiness". Here again, we see the glory of God as a mysterious reality that breaks into human experience as a transforming, intense, transcendent, and awe-inspiring presence.

[1] Romans 1:21–22; 3:7; 8:18; and Isaiah 6:1–8.

Think of Peter when he makes the miraculous catch of fish and falls at the feet of Jesus, John on Mount Tabor when he encounters the Transfiguration of the Lord, Mary at the moment of the Annunciation, or Stephen when he sees the heavens open up and the Son of Man seated at the right hand of the Father.

Can we not say, then, that the glory of God is the light, power, love, grace, mercy, and joy that radiate from the very being of the Divine Mystery? Although the people of the Old Testament could not look upon God and live, the coming of the Lord in the human flesh of Christ, the Son of God, enables us to gaze upon the face of Jesus and encounter there the fullness of God's presence and glory, inextricably bound up in our own human flesh and earthly reality.

Since we cannot fully experience God in the pure essence of His unapproachable divinity, He pours His glory and life upon the Son, who is both human and divine, so that we can find Him in Jesus. This desire of God fully to reveal Himself captures the meaning of Advent and Christmas.

Where have you and I experienced the weight and the light of the *shekinah*, the mysterious divine presence? Sometimes, I find it helpful to write my encounters of the glory of God in a journal and then go back to them, sometimes years later. Such memories often serve as signposts on the curving and mysterious path to the Kingdom of God.

Knowing without the shadow of a doubt that I met the Lord here in that person or there in that moment consoles me in those inevitable times of trial, temptation, and doubt. Where does the *shekinah* dwell in your home, family, marriage, workplace, and heart?

I remember particular encounters in the Sacrament of Reconciliation when I confessed something heavy and difficult, feeling the burden lifted by the extraordinary mercy of God. Sometimes when I am consecrating the bread and wine at Mass, I feel the glory of God manifest in the Eucharist as both weight and light, the *shekinah* radically present in both the sacred species on the altar and the People of God gathered around in prayer.

Conversations with thousands of people throughout my life in which individuals shared their deepest hopes, struggles, sins, and joys revealed the wondrous presence of the Holy Spirit working in varied ways in so many lives. Once in a while, I feel the *kavod* of the Lord's presence in prayer, when my restless thoughts, inadequate words, and fleeting emotions fall away, even for just a few seconds, and I encounter the depths of God in the silence and darkness of my fragile, quavering soul. Walking in the woods on a sunny autumn day, hearing only a gentle wind and crackling leaves under my feet, wrapped in the mystery of God's world, is another glorious moment.

What are your *shekinah* experiences when God was so close that you could have touched Him or you felt the nearness of the divine breath? Write them down.

Saint Paul reminds us that we are created to glorify God, to refract back, as if in a mirror, the love, mercy, grace, and joy we have come to know so that others, too, can encounter the glory of the Lord and live in the practice of faith and good works. We glorify and praise God when we increasingly become the saints who He called us to be from the beginning. As Saint Irenaeus said, "For the glory of God is a living man; and the life of man consists in beholding God."[2]

---

[2] *Adversus Haereses*, bk. 4, chap. 20, trans. Alexander Roberts and William Rambaut, from *Ante-Nicene Fathers*, vol. 1, eds. Alexander Roberts, James Donaldson, and A. Cleveland Coxe (Buffalo, NY: Christian Literature Publishing, 1885). Revised and edited for New Advent by Kevin Knight, http://www.newadvent.org/fathers/0103420.htm.

At the end of his first trip to Mexico in 1979, Saint John Paul II boarded his plane in Mexico City and took off for the return flight to Rome. As the plane ascended, he looked down and saw an astonishing ocean of light! The tens of thousands who had gathered to see him off brought along mirrors, holding them to the sun as a gesture of final farewell. The pope was moved to tears.

Maybe that is what it means to glorify God: to hold our lives up to the light, as a mirror to the sun, reflecting back the mercy, love, and peace that we have received.

We hold this treasure in earthen vessels.

Part 2

God's Love Is Revealed through Service

Discover the Radiance of the Soul

One day I had the joy and blessing of accompanying Mother Teresa's Missionaries of Charity sisters in their home visits. We visited a young man who was completely paralyzed in bed because of injuries he suffered ten years ago when he saved the life of a drowning girl. We saw a young mother who raises her children well despite many physical and material obstacles in her life. We talked with a young woman who, despite being wheelchair bound, finds joy in the love of family and friends who surround her. That night, I had dinner with a beautiful young family whose husband and father has ALS (amyotrophic lateral sclerosis).

In all of these amazing people I encountered the living Christ! None of them felt sorry for themselves, expressed anger, or even seemed sad. All of them had worked through the mystery and tragedy of their chronic suffering and had come to a sacred place of peace and acceptance. All of them spoke of the meaning of Jesus' Cross and the hope that faith and prayer give them. It was truly a blessed day.

Each of these remarkable encounters teaches me the dignity and beauty of human life. People can live in the most difficult and painful circumstances, endure chronic suffering beyond imagination, experience heartbreaking setbacks and tragedies, and yet, still triumph in love and hope. Faith in the Lord, who suffers with us in tender compassion and carries us in the transforming power of His Sacred Heart and shows us even now the glory of eternal life, is the secret to such astonishing victories.

I can't help but contrast such inspiring human transcendence with the dark and terrible realities that afflict our nation and world. We were all horrified to watch the Planned Parenthood videos in which people callously spoke about selling body parts of aborted children over a lunch of pasta and laughter. And many of our leaders not only tolerate such evil but defend it. The murder rate in many of our cities is sky-high; so much of it is related to gangs, drugs, poverty, and children who grew up in a culture of violence and lovelessness. Isis and other terrorist groups continue to inflict torture, destruction, and butchery upon the world; thousands of people have been killed because of their faith in Jesus Christ, and thousands more have been driven from their homes, losing everything they ever possessed as they flee for their lives. More people seem to be slipping into poverty, as low-income wages keep them from ever breaking the vicious cycle that traps them.

As followers of Jesus crucified and risen, we embrace the Gospel that offers the fullness of salvation, joy, meaning, justice, and mercy, not only in the next life, but right here and right now. The tenor of our times demands that we make a fundamental choice over and over again: the decision to live for God, to embrace our own dignity as a daughter or son of the Father, to act consciously to lift up those around us, to embrace virtue, prayer, good works, and love as the very meaning of our existence. Despite some great strides in human rights, respect, and dignity, we cannot remain morally neutral in a world that still remains way too mired in racism, poverty, violence, ignorance of God, and a fundamental misunderstanding of the glory and vocation of the human person.

When I think of all the people I encountered with the Sisters of Charity, starting with the sisters at Mass at 7:00 A.M. and ending with a joyful family dinner, I realize that every single one of them radiated God, goodness, life, and joy. It was almost as if they were turned inside out, and I could see the beauty and light of their souls. In *The Way of Perfection*, Saint Teresa of Ávila puts it this way, "Well, let us imagine that within us is an extremely rich palace, built entirely of gold and precious stones; in sum, built for a lord such as this. Imagine, too, as is indeed so, that you have a part to play in order for the palace to be so beautiful; for there is no edifice as beautiful as is a soul pure and full of virtues. The greater the virtues the more resplendent the jewels. Imagine, also, that in this palace dwells this mighty King who has been gracious enough to become your Father; and that he is seated upon an extremely valuable throne, which is your heart."[1] In *The Interior Castle*, she goes on to compare the human soul to the Tree of Life at the center of the Garden of Eden and the burning bush that attracts the attention of Moses.[2] God is fundamentally closer to us than we are to ourselves, so to discover God we must go deeply within and there discover the radiance of the soul, this "Interior Castle" made of crystal and shining with the glory of God.

How different our world would be if everyone could recognize this substantial truth: the dignity and worth of every human being, created in the image and likeness of God, made to love and be loved, destined for eternal life, and shining more wondrously than the rising sun! This

---

[1] Teresa of Ávila, *The Way of Perfection: Study Edition* (Washington, D.C.: ICS Publications, 2000), p. 303.

[2] Teresa of Ávila, *The Interior* Castle, trans. Benedictines of Stanbrook (Oil City, Penn.: Baronius Press, 2015), p. 130.

vision of the Kingdom of God, imbedded in the mystery of human flesh, explains the truth, beauty, and goodness of both Jesus Christ and ourselves. As Saint Paul says, we hold "this treasure in earthen vessels".[3] What a treasure! What a vessel!

[3] 2 Cor 4:7.

Illuminate the Darkness

Archbishop Saint Oscar Romero and Dorothy Day, two contemporary icons of Catholic social teaching, have much to teach us about applying the ideals of the Gospel to concrete situations of poverty and injustice.

In her early years, Dorothy Day was both an agnostic and a Communist who was passionately dedicated to bettering the plight of the poor and workers in the early decades of the twentieth century. Her ultimate conversion to Catholicism only enhanced her commitment to social transformation. Together with Peter Maurin, a Frenchman deeply immersed in philosophy, she founded the Catholic Worker Movement, setting up hospitality houses where Catholics lived together in voluntary poverty and served the neediest through the corporal works of mercy. Day was also a radical pacifist who spoke out fearlessly against war and violence.

Oscar Romero, a timid and shy churchman, became the Archbishop of El Salvador during that country's terrible civil war in the 1970s. As he witnessed the military dictatorship's brutal oppression of his people, the torture and murder of priests who spoke out against the government, and the deep economic injustices of a corrupt system, Romero became a courageous prophet for the dispossessed, calling for peace, an end to the violence, and a just political order. He was murdered by government soldiers while celebrating Mass in 1980.

These two powerful Christian witnesses demonstrate the need for us to apply and put into practice the teachings of Christ and the Church in all aspects of human reality, both personal and social. As long as such teachings safely remain as words on a page of the Bible or the *Catechism*, no one feels rattled or threatened by them. We can all pay lip service to the noble ideals of the dignity of the human person, the need for a just social order, and the integrity of sexuality, as long as it all remains theoretical and detached from real life.

But, as serious Christians, we can never stay safely attached to the merely theoretical; our Catholic faith sends us into this world that is marred and warped by sin, violence, poverty, lust, despair, and greed, in order to apply the doctrines of the Church to living people, concrete situations, and social structures. When we actually start acting the Gospel out in the lived reality of economics, politics, and culture, we start getting into trouble.

When I served in the Dominican Republic, no one took issue with our parish building latrines, teaching people to read, or dispensing food and medicine, but when we formed a human rights committee, started working on needed land reform, and talked about the rights and needs of the campesinos, a group of government soldiers with guns came to the rectory one day to question me about what we were doing.

When we start helping to free persons from the evil clutches of human trafficking, those who profit from prostitution and sweat shops will get angry. When we attempt to help women in crisis pregnancies to choose for the life in their wombs, the lucrative abortion industry will come after us. When we question the ethics and greed of Wall Street, some will call us Communists. When we defend religious freedom and the integrity of marriage, some will call us "haters" or "intolerant". When we stand up against the death penalty, some will label us "naïve" or "soft".

None of this opposition should deter us from living our faith in the concrete situations of our society; sometimes such criticism can actually be a stamp of approval that we are living our Gospel values. As Jesus said, "Woe to you, when all men speak well of you, for so their fathers did to the false prophets."[1] Embracing the teachings of Christ can be a subversive activity, because when we follow the Lord, He uses us to overthrow the deceptions, injustices, hatred, and sin of this world and to help the Kingdom of God to flourish with greater authenticity and power.

Oscar Romero, Dorothy Day, Maximilian Kolbe, Mother Teresa, and Francis of Assisi, as well as countless other Christians, show us by the power of their example the practicality of the Gospel. Jesus' teachings simply remain words on a page until we specifically apply them to real people and actual situations. G. K. Chesterton famously said in his *What's Wrong with the World* that "Christianity cannot be condemned because it has not yet been fully tried." Peter Maurin said that "the Gospel is a keg of dynamite that Christians have been sitting on for two thousand years."[2]

We ask the Lord to inspire us to go ever deeper into our faith, to make our love more specific and practical, and to allow the Lord's generous sacrifice on the Cross to move our hearts to be that lavish in our response to His astonishing mercy. The world needs the light of Christ more than ever; we are called to illuminate the darkness of the world!

---

[1] Lk 6:26.
[2] Peter Maurin, *Easy Essays* (Chicago: Franciscan Herald Press, 1977), 3.

The Lord Is Awaiting Us

A simple but profound way to live is to practice the corporal and spiritual works of mercy. The corporal works include feed the hungry, give drink to the thirsty, clothe the naked, shelter the homeless, visit the sick and the imprisoned, and bury the dead. These simple actions of kindness and love are the litmus test for those admitted into the Kingdom of Heaven in chapter 25 of the Gospel of Matthew.

The complete identification between the Son of God and the poor and suffering is truly astonishing. In Jesus' ministry of preaching and healing, He is the one who offers mercy to the sinner, feeds the hungry, and lifts up the sick and the dead, serving from a position of strength and power. Then, in the Passion and Cross, a profound subversion takes place. Jesus becomes the prisoner, the thirsty one, the naked person, even the dead man. He moves from a position of strength to weakness, from the one offering mercy and healing to the one seemingly in need of it.

This radical shift adds a new dimension to the mystery and presence of God in the world. While we still pray to the Lord for graces, blessings, healing, and even miracles, we also find God in the broken, the hopeless, the suffering,

This is a modified version of an article originally published as "Living the Works of Mercy", *Northwest Indiana Catholic* (website), January 17, 2016, https://www.nwicatholic.com/index.php/2011-10-28-15-52-16/bishop-hying -column?start=147.

and the marginalized. While Jesus dispenses God's mercy through His death and Resurrection, through the Church and the sacraments, He also is in need of that same mercy in the distressing disguise of the poor. He offers us life, blessing, and peace, but also begs those same gifts from us, as we share with the most marginalized and needy.

The great secret of the saints' extraordinary holiness and love was their ability literally to see Christ in the suffering, the sick, and the poor. Mother Teresa, picking up that first man out of Calcutta's gutter; Francis of Assisi, kissing the leper; Vincent de Paul, seeking out the poor in the slums of Paris; and countless others have experienced the radiant presence of Christ in the darkest, dirtiest, and most unexpected places—the lives of the most vulnerable and forgotten.

I had one such experience during my mission time in the Dominican Republic. The government there converted a soldiers' barracks located in our parish boundaries into a prison. These four simple buildings around an open square, constructed for a hundred soldiers, now housed four hundred prisoners. The food was awful; the plumbing didn't work; there were no classes, books, games, or television; and the merciless sun beat down on them every day. Young boys and old men, folks with mental illness and disease, and killers and the innocent all lived in these squalid conditions, day in and out, with little hope of freedom or justice.

We started celebrating Mass there every week, first through the bars and then inside the big open square. I will never forget a particular Eucharist I offered on a particular August 6, the Feast of the Transfiguration, the time on Mount Tabor when Jesus is momentarily glorified in the radiant light of the Resurrection. As I celebrated the Mass that day in the middle of the heat, bugs, smell, chaos, and despair, I experienced something that I can only define as mystical.

For a moment, during the Eucharistic Prayer, it was as if all those disturbing particulars that defined these men's lives had fallen away and I could see them as God sees them: precious, radiant, and beloved children of the Father. I felt like we had all passed over to the glory of Heaven for just a few minutes.

When we reach out to others, by putting the works of mercy into practice, we literally touch, feed, shelter, console, and serve Christ Himself. These important works of mercy and charity make the Gospel come alive, both for us and for the people we serve.

When we perform such Christlike actions with great love, God uses us to unleash powerfully in this place and time with these people the Paschal Mystery—the death and Resurrection of Christ.

The spiritual works of mercy include instruct the ignorant, counsel the doubtful, admonish sinners, bear wrongs patiently, forgive offenses, comfort the afflicted, and pray for the living and the dead. These works allow us to bring God's mercy into our homes, schools, workplaces, and neighborhoods. Our families may not need food or clothing, but who doesn't need comfort and forgiveness? Our classmates may not be homeless, but sometimes they hurt us or are hurting themselves and we can be Christ for them. All of us can pray for others, no matter where we are.

The Lord is quietly and patiently awaiting us in the disguise of every person we meet. What a privilege to love Christ in this way, to assuage His terrible thirst for our mercy and attention.

Pierce the Veil and See Only Christ

As Pope Francis has reminded us in many ways, mercy is at the very heart of the Christian mystery. Jesus comes to the rescue of fallen and lost humanity to save us from sin and death. Mercy is love in action or how a good and generous heart responds when confronted by misery and suffering.

Saint Faustina Kowalska, a Polish nun of the twentieth century, experienced visions of Jesus revealing His Divine Mercy to her, later published as *The Diary of Saint Maria Faustina Kowalska: Divine Mercy in My Soul*. He calls all people to trust in the love of the Father, to embrace forgiveness and reconciliation, to leave sin and fear behind, and to live the Good News of the Gospel as a new creation. How telling that Saint Faustina received these messages just a few years before the outbreak of World War II, a global catastrophe of demonic inhumanity and unspeakable suffering. It is as if the Lord was preparing the world for what was to come, reminding us that only the path of justice, love, and mercy can forge a true, lasting peace and a humane social order.

How do we embrace this Divine Mercy in our lives?

In the sacraments, God pours the grace of His love and presence into our spirits, so the more we celebrate the sacraments of the Eucharist and Reconciliation, the closer we come to the very Heart of God. Deep personal prayer, meditation on the Scriptures, praying the Rosary and the Divine Mercy Chaplet, embracing silence and peace as we can throughout the day—such experiences help us to know and feel the love of God as a living and pulsating reality; the Sacred Heart beats at the very center of the universe, and *we* are part of that Mystical Body.

We need to pray often for the vision of the saints who were literally able to see Christ in every person they encountered. Mercy allows us to pierce the veil that hides the radiant presence of the Lord in others. Love helps us to look beyond the faults, weaknesses, poverty, and unattractiveness in others that often keep us at a distance from them and to see only Christ.

Such a spiritual view sounds easy but is often difficult in practice! How pleasant it is to associate with the beautiful, successful, and popular people, the ones who agree with us or think we are wonderful or don't make us uncomfortable. How difficult to love truly those who malign us behind our backs, usually seem unpleasant and disagreeable, or are simply uninteresting—those who seemingly have nothing to offer us, so that giving them attention and love will bring nothing back to us.

These encounters are where mercy kicks into practice, where love exceeds what appears to be just, reasonable, and appropriate. How do we practice mercy within our families? Often, we can show kindness to others outside, but then at home, the façade can drop and we let out all of our anger, indifference, and resentment on the people we love the most because it seems safe; they "have" to take it.

Can we give our spouses, children, parents, brothers, and sisters another chance? A friend of mine recently wrote a letter to his brother from whom he has been estranged for years, simply asking for forgiveness and promising love and prayers. Now is the perfect time to heal broken relationships, especially within the family.

Can we be merciful at work? We all seem to have a coworker who gets on our nerves, wastes time, gossips, or is actively hostile. Such folks are usually deeply wounded themselves, acting out their own inner pain and anger, inflicting it on others in some unconscious attempt to feel better. Do we have the courage to draw near their suffering, even at the risk of enduring some of the hurt?

This analogy may limp a little, but I think we Christians are called to be like water filters, absorbing the dirt and impurities of the world and becoming like overflowing fountains of love and goodness that quench the world's terrible thirst for mercy and acceptance. I have never met a person who did not crave more love, attention, kindness, and affirmation, which is another way of saying that everyone is looking for God, whether they know it or not. Can we be that life-giving fountain that waters the parched soil of humanity with mercy?

Mercy comes down to little things: how we drive on the highway and when we thank people for favors received, apologize and admit error and weakness, listen to people, even when it isn't interesting, volunteer to serve the poor and sick, give money to charity, express joy in the face of adversity, bear wrongs patiently, and show kindness to unlikeable people, as well as when we do not insist on our way and do not complain. None of these things will win us applause and fame, but they will build up the Kingdom of God. When we let the mercy of God into our lives, we will know conversion and will increasingly become instruments of mercy in the lives of others, leading them to the Lord. How beautiful to see the wonders of God's goodness in motion all around us!

Spiritually and Physically Fed

Christ calls all of us to practice with greater generosity and zeal the corporal and spiritual works of mercy, acting out the script of the Gospel with passion and purpose.

In Matthew 25, Jesus reminds us that we will be judged on how we love and serve the poor and the needy. We see in the lives of so many of the saints the exciting results when Christians take the Good News literally and let the Holy Spirit lead them to love the marginalized with the very heart of Christ.

Think of all the people who have fed you throughout your life! Mothers and fathers, grandparents, cafeteria cooks, good friends, and restaurant chefs have all fed us thousands of meals, nourishing both our bodies and spirits with comfort food that gives life and love.

Our planet has enough food to sustain all of the billions of us, but due to poverty, war, waste, corruption, and lack of transportation, many people still suffer malnutrition and starvation. Feeding the hungry is a basic human action that Christ has lifted up as a work of mercy for our brothers and sisters. Everyone has a right to eat in order to sustain life, health, and energy.

After serving in the Dominican Republic, where many people eat once a day, I can no longer look at good and wonderful food being thrown in the garbage without feeling sadness and regret for the plight of our hungry brothers and sisters across the planet.

Across the nation, scores of food pantries, meal programs, and soup kitchens serve the hungry in our midst.

Parishes, schools, and Saint Vincent de Paul conferences sponsor many of these wonderful efforts, fueled by thousands of people who donate time, money, and food. Please consider helping in this remarkable service of love if you have not yet done so. No loving action can be more needed, basic, and life-giving than to feed another person.

Ponder the famous quote from Gandhi, the Hindu leader of the Indian people who achieved freedom through non-violence, through the lens of both the Eucharist and feeding the hungry: "There are people in the world so hungry that God cannot appear to them except in the form of bread."

This question reminds us that the Lord feeds us with His Body and Blood, nourishing our souls with the saving divine presence that leads us to eternal life, just as He multiplied bread and fish to sustain the hungry multitude in the wilderness. In feeding us both spiritually and physically, God gives us the energy and resources to pass on the gift to those who hunger for bread, affection, justice, love, and peace.

Recognize the Flicker of Divine Spark

A better way to express the thought behind "Instruct the ignorant" may be "Teach and form others." Ponder all the people who have taught, educated, and formed you to be the person you are today. Our parents, teachers, catechists, coaches, pastors, and friends have all molded our character, formed our intellect, taught us the faith, inspired us to love and give, and led us down our vocational path.

I remember the names of all of my teachers in school from kindergarten forward, as well as catechists, priests, sisters, coaches, and Scout leaders, because each one had a deep impact on my life. I praise God for all the people who dedicate their lives to educating and forming our young people. I particularly thank the hundreds of school teachers, catechists, priests, deacons, and religious who form us in the faith, so that we can know, love, and follow the Lord Jesus Christ.

Opportunities abound to step forward and impact our precious young people in beautiful and formative ways. Our religious education programs, Scouts, Boys and Girls Clubs, Big Brothers and Big Sisters and Best Buddies are just some of the wonderful ways that we can help love and mentor children.

Many young people suffer intensely the feeling that no one cares about them, nurtures them, or loves them. When we are not mothered and fathered properly, a hole in the heart and a longing in the soul can damage us emotionally, psychologically, and spiritually. How many people in our world are deeply wounded because they were not loved and nurtured as children? When we generously step forward to volunteer, when we love and form our own children and grandchildren, when we teach, catechize, coach, and mentor, another precious human life flourishes and grows in the warm sun of our attention and affection.

Is there a greater gift that we can offer another than to share our faith in Jesus Christ and the love in our hearts?

As the Body of Christ, we serve the dignity of everyone, recognizing the flicker of that divine spark that burns in every heart and mind. Mercy calls us to sacrifice ourselves for the sake of those near and far who are starving for food, love, and joy.

Transform the World

One of the best-kept secrets of the Catholic Church is the richness of her social teaching, her broad and expansive vision of the human person and the justice, peace, mercy, rights, and responsibilities that flow from the reality of the Kingdom of God as a properly ordered communion of love and goodness. The 1971 Synod of Bishops, dedicated to building justice and peace in the world, declared in their document "Justice in the World" that the struggle for justice is a "constitutive dimension of the preaching of the Gospel".

When I did mission work in the Dominican Republic, the president of the country visited our parish once during the election season and attended Mass. He was in the communion line, right behind a poor little boy who was dirty and barefoot. They lived in different worlds but, at that moment, they were radically one—brothers in the Body of Christ, equally loved and important.

The fact that one went back to his palace and the other to a hut reveals the injustice and sin of the world, but more importantly, how our experience of the Eucharist is the source of the Catholic vision for the social order. The Lord calls us to transform the world so that our politics, economy, culture, and community reflect the justice, peace, mercy, and joy that we experience at Mass.

Catholic social teaching embraces seven basic principles that serve as a foundation for all of our work to transform the world into a civilization of love.

The first and most fundamental one is a profound respect for the dignity of the human person.

Created in the image and likeness of God, redeemed by the precious Blood of Christ, every single person has an absolute value as a child of the Father. This conviction roots the Church's passion to protect and lift up the unborn, children, the elderly, the poor, the sick, and the disabled, as well as all who are marginalized and fragile. No one can ever treat another person as a thing or a means to an end.

Every person has rights and responsibilities, including the right to life, food, education, culture, health care, and free speech, as well as participation in society and politics and work and freedom from violence and abuse. We also have the responsibility to work, contribute to the common good, vote, serve others, especially the marginalized, and respect the lives of others. Our individualized American culture often seems more comfortable asserting rights than responsibilities and the common good. The Church holds up both as necessary and pivotal.

The call to community and active participation in the life of society is an integral part of being fully human. We are not isolated individuals living in a vacuum, but rather brothers and sisters who benefit from and contribute to a richly complex network of social relationships.

Marriage and family is the primary human community in which each individual becomes fully human through a communion of love, service, faith, and sharing. In this context of the common good, the dignity of work and the rights of workers is a fundamental component. In our Catholic tradition, work is not simply a necessary evil but rather a sacred action of service that participates in the creative work of God Himself. Economy, production, and work all flourish to serve the needs of the human person, not the other way around.

As followers of Christ, we are called to serve the most vulnerable and needy sacrificially, giving what we can so that everyone can live his full humanity with dignity and joy. Saint Pope John Paul II and now Pope Francis have reflected often on the virtue of solidarity and the preferential option for the poor. The Catholic Church feeds more hungry people, cares for more sick people, educates more children, and serves more persons who are trapped in poverty than any other institution on earth. We do this because we see ourselves as servants of the human person, who was created by God and redeemed by Christ.

Another integral part of Catholic social teaching, connected to our love for the poor, is a concentrated care for the environment, the beautiful world of nature that God has entrusted to us as a sacred obligation of stewardship and fruitfulness.

When I witness the remarkable variety and quantity of good work done by people who generously and perseveringly live out our Catholic social doctrine, I feel amazed, inspired, and grateful. From meal programs and food pantries to prison ministry and care for the sick, from defending life in the womb to defending life on death row, from building up marriages and families to advocating for the unemployed and the homeless—our parishes, schools, youth, priests, deacons, religious orders, lay faithful, Catholic Charities, Saint Vincent de Paul, Knights of Columbus, and countless others, both inside the Church and alongside her, daily build up the Kingdom of God, create a civilization of love, add to the joy, love, mercy, and justice in the world, and help to narrow the gap between the life we experience in the Eucharist and the reality of our society.

My fervent prayer is that we will be inspired to do even greater and bolder things for the glory of God and His beloved poor.

A Transcendent Witness

It would be hard to imagine the Catholic Church without the uplifting presence, radiant witness, and dedicated contribution of consecrated virgins, hermits, and religious.

The Church benefits from the fruitful life of so many religious communities who founded and serve a rich variety of schools, hospitals, nursing homes, and social services. If we factored out the enormous contribution of consecrated life from the history of our cities and state, we would see a gaping hole in education, health care, and service to the poor and vulnerable. Throughout the history of the Church, religious orders produced saints, kept ancient learning alive, founded thousands of monasteries and convents, created universities and hospitals, and developed better farming methods—in all things producing order and civilization in many situations where there was none.

If we only look at what consecrated persons do, however, we would be missing the central point of such a purposeful way of living. By embracing the vows of poverty, chastity, and obedience, the consecrated give radical and profound witness to Jesus Christ, who Himself was poor, chaste, and obedient to the Father. Such a life points beyond the material and physical limits of this world toward the Kingdom of God and the saving truth of the Gospel. In his being, a consecrated person is a transcendent witness who reminds us that only God is eternal, that this life is fleeting, and that our hearts need to be fixed on the good things of Heaven.

In a culture that often turns the gift of our sexuality into lustful promiscuity, the consecrated person vows to live celibate chastity in order to love God and others freely. In a society that often loves things and uses people, the consecrated vow themselves to poverty. In a world that equates freedom with license, the consecrated promise obedience to God and their superiors. These vows are a conscious renunciation of the ephemeral in order to be free to embrace the eternal and holy life of Christ, lived in the mystery of the Church.

An ancient way of life, going all the way back to the Scriptures, consecrated virginity gives radical witness to Jesus Christ as our true good. Women who take such a vow live in the world, working in a secular profession and belonging to a parish. Their spirituality is profoundly spousal, viewing Jesus as the Bridegroom and love of their lives. In this way, consecrated virgins live out the union between Christ and the Church.

Hermits live in solitude, not as a renunciation of other people or the world, but rather to love the Lord free of distraction, finding God in the silence of a life wholly given over to meditation and contemplation. Many of the saints, including Benedict, Scholastica, Anthony of the Desert, and Julian of Norwich, spent time apart, dwelling in caves or huts, far from the noise and distraction of the world. Hermits live out the solitude of the Lord, who spent many nights in prayer alone with the Father.

Religious live the consecrated life in community as brother or sister disciples in the Lord Jesus, giving witness to the Gospel through their common life of faith, charity, and prayer, acting out the specific charism of their founder. The number and variety of religious orders, the reach of their apostolic activity, and the transformative difference they make in the world is truly a wonder and a gift to celebrate. One can find women and men religious in the poorest, most obscure, and difficult human situations. Third World slum dwellers, prisoners on death row, orphans, the homeless, victims of AIDS, the elderly, the abandoned, schoolchildren, and the poor all find mercy and hope because of the love and service of Catholic religious.

We give thanks to God for the gift of Jesus Christ, His salvation, the mystery of the Church, and, in a special way, the legacy and service of consecrated persons in the world, the Church, and our lives. All of us are better Catholics and better people because of the example and goodness of countless sisters, brothers, priests, virgins, and hermits who have loved, prayed, and mentored us into Christian discipleship.

The Saints of World Youth Day

I was blessed to join hundreds of thousands of Catholics from all over the world to celebrate, witness, and grow in our faith at the 2016 World Youth Day in Poland with Pope Francis.

Conceived by Pope John Paul II, World Youth Day is an event that lasts six days, is held usually every three years in a different country, and is intended to increase the faith and love of Catholic young people. Skeptics in the Vatican never thought an event of such magnitude could ever succeed, but, as so often was the case, Saint John Paul II proved his critics wrong.

I have participated in three World Youth Days prior to the 2016 event in Poland—Denver in 1993, Toronto in 2002, and Cologne in 2005. All intense experiences, these encounters offer times for Mass, reconciliation and prayer, catechetical sessions with our bishops, service experiences with the poor and sick, music, fun, and touring around, all of which culminate in a long walk to a massive field on Saturday in preparation for a prayer service with the Holy Father that night.

Then, everybody sleeps overnight in the field, and the next morning the pope returns to celebrate a huge closing Mass with all the pilgrims. Such a trek is not for the faint of heart! It involves long travel; much walking; tolerating heat, crowds, sleeplessness, a lot of waiting, and limited bathroom facilities. But it is a pilgrimage and everybody loves it!

Saint John Paul II clearly intuited that we as Catholics can't just live our faith in our heads all the time, just thinking about God or creating this privatized world of just Jesus and me. Because the Son of God became incarnate in our flesh, we need to see, hear, feel, act, sing, and even sometimes shout out our faith, in communion with other people, both within the Church and in the world.

If our practice of religion ever becomes so antiseptic that we never get our hands dirty because of it, are never inconvenienced in some big ways, never live it out in broader contexts that make us feel uncomfortable, or never cry or laugh because of it, we are not yet fully disciples of the Lord Jesus.

When you read the Acts of the Apostles or the lives of the saints, you realize quickly that these spiritual leaders rejoiced, bled, sweated, cried, suffered, danced, laughed, sacrificed, and worked hard—and were even sometimes killed to build the Kingdom of God. Faith was a tangible, gritty reality because Jesus Christ was real, alive, and present in all the details of their lives.

Pilgrimages, mission trips, processions, hands-on service, devotions, vacation Bible camps, World Youth Days, and a multitude of other experiences make Catholicism a beautiful and wild patchwork quilt of encounters with the power of the divine presence, mysteriously imbedded in the complexity of the human experience.

Young people are unfailingly transformed through their participation in World Youth Days because they fundamentally grasp this truth on a very deep level. Many married couples, singles, priests, and religious discovered their vocations because of World Youth Day!

Coming back from Denver, Toronto, Cologne, or Poland, young people would tell me that they never knew the Church was so big or diverse, that there were so many other young people like themselves living the faith, that being Catholic could be this much fun, that God loved them so much, or that their lives and what they do really matter so much.

Occurring in the context of the Jubilee Year of Mercy, World Youth Day in Poland focused on the extraordinary love of God, poured out in the life, ministry, death, and Resurrection of Jesus Christ. As we collectively live through this very difficult historical moment, fraught with terrorism, violence, mass killings, hatred, rage, poverty, and war, the world has never needed the saving, healing, reconciling, and forgiving mercy of Jesus Christ more.

As disciples of the Lord Jesus in this troubled time, we are the instruments of that mercy and peace. This realization simultaneously inspires, frightens, energizes, overwhelms, and ultimately reassures me that the Gospel call is authentic, life-giving, and transformative when we have the courage and grace to respond. God is with us and is the one who does all the heavy lifting.

The World Youth Day event in Poland culminated in a field outside the city, as a million-plus pilgrims gathered on Saturday night to keep vigil with the Holy Father. A memory that will always live in my heart is the adoration of the Eucharist as this massive crowd knelt in the field, holding candles in the setting sun, honoring the Eucharistic Christ.

In every direction, all the way to the horizon, all you could see were thousands and thousands of candles! People from every country, language, culture, and place were all united in the love of Christ and the Church. The power of love triumphs in a place where the evil systems of both the Nazis and the Soviets tried to stamp out religious practice and destroy human dignity.

On that unforgettable Saturday night, the pope spoke powerfully to the world's youth; he was on the top of his game. Here is an excerpt: "Dear young people, we didn't come into this work to 'vegetate', to take it easy, to make our lives a comfortable sofa to fall asleep on. No, we came for another reason: to leave a mark.... But when we opt for ease and convenience, for confusing happiness with consumption, then we end up paying a high price indeed: we lose our freedom."[1]

The Holy Father called us to wake up spiritually, to be protagonists of history, to follow the disciples out of the Upper Room on Pentecost, and to give our lives to the flourishing of the reign of God and the proclamation of the Gospel.

So many forces in our culture want us to fall asleep, to stay numb and drugged, to disengage from life, and to sit passively on the sidelines, playing our video games and staying in front of the computer for hours on end.

"That is probably the most harmful and insidious form of paralysis.... Because, little by little, without even realizing it, we start to nod off, to grow drowsy and dull ... while others—perhaps more alert than we are, but not necessarily better—decide our future for us," the pope said. "For many people in fact, it is much easier and better to have drowsy and dull kids who confuse happiness with a sofa. For many people, that is more convenient than having young people who are alert and searching, trying to respond to God's dream and to all the restlessness present in the human heart."

So how do we stay spiritually awake and vigilant, ready to open the door when the Bridegroom knocks in the third watch of the night as Saint Luke's Gospel tells us in chapter 12?

[1] This excerpt and the following are from the Vatican's website at http://www.vatican.va/content/francesco/en/speeches/2016/july/documents/papa-francesco_20160730_polonia-veglia-giovani.html.

Several things I try to practice to stay alert include Scripture, sacrifice, and Confession. You may have other methods or ways of staying on the spiritual beam, but these work for me.

In reading the Scriptures for Mass and in praying the Liturgy of the Hours, I encounter the Word regularly. Each day, I look for a word, a phrase, an image, or a thought from the Bible that I can carry with me. It could be "mercy" or "The Lord is my shepherd" or the woman at the well or Moses at the burning bush. I try to ponder that image or word throughout the day and to see everyone and everything I experience through that scriptural prism. This practice helps me stay focused. Imagine if we used Scripture the way we use our smartphones.

I try to do something sacrificially kind for someone every day, whether I think they deserve it or not, whether I feel like doing it or not. It could take the form of a phone call, a text, a visit, or a gift, as well as a word of encouragement or praise or helping with a simple task. These little things, which are sometimes so miniscule that they go unnoticed, put together with millions of other small acts of kindness and charity can change the world! At least they change me, expanding my heart and my capacity to give. We are here to learn how to love, to *really* love, generously, joyfully, and sacrificially.

I try to go to Confession regularly. This sacrament helps me to feel the mercy of God, the power of forgiveness, and my need for conversion. Confessing helps me take stock of my life, admit my failure, acknowledge my need for salvation and love, and go out renewed in the mission of Christ. Find a good confessor to whom you can open your heart. The Lord works so powerfully when we open up our weaknesses and need. Love and mercy heal us, enabling us to become living icons of the merciful Father in the Parable of the Prodigal Son.

We ask the Lord to keep waking, challenging, consoling, bothering, and prodding us, so that we resist the urge to settle for complacency, stay in a comfortable fog, and fall asleep on the couch. So much work of the Kingdom lies before us. As Robert Frost put it in the last two lines of his poem "Stopping by Woods on a Snowy Evening", "I have miles to go before I sleep."

In Poland, we were elated, inspired, tired, joyful, impatient, hungry, challenged, nourished, and sanctified. We experienced deep moments of prayer, communion, love, peace, and also craziness, exhaustion, and confusion. God does amazing things in and around us.Sounds a lot like the lives of the saints!

Every Catholic Is Called to Evangelize

Four Signs of a Dynamic Catholic by Matthew Kelly, first published in 2012, is one of my favorite books. Kelly is an effective inspiration in the Catholic Church, speaking and writing about the need to live our faith with greater passion and purpose. Several years ago, I was privileged to hear him speak on the *Four Signs* book and was so fired up that I bought five thousand copies to give away. Matthew emailed me to find out what I was going to do with all those books! So if you want to get an author's attention, just buy a bunch of their books.

Four Signs begins with a surprising statistic: 7 percent of U.S. Catholics do 80 percent of the volunteering, serving, leading, and contributing. Based on my pastoral experience, I would say this number is accurate. In a typical parish, usually about one hundred to two hundred people do just about everything. This statistical discovery prompted Matthew Kelly to interview thousands of Catholics across the country who fell into the 7 percent category to see what makes them tick and what common qualities they exhibit that make them so highly engaged in the practice of their faith. The book is an articulation of the four common characteristics of these dynamic Catholics.

The first sign is a firm, faithful, and disciplined dedication to regular prayer. Dynamic Catholics pray every day, usually at the same time and place. Maybe it's reading Scripture over a cup of coffee first thing in the morning, praying the

Rosary during a power walk, daily Mass and time before the Blessed Sacrament, or using a guided meditation before bed. Many Catholics pray in moments of trial and stress or before meals or a quick prayer before they go to sleep, but not as many have a dedicated and passionate conversation with God that occurs every day. This may be because many people have never really been taught how to pray or they tried one method and it didn't work.

If you are looking to deepen your prayer life, talk to your pastor or someone you know who really prays and get their input, or just start meditating on one of the Gospels or buy one of those little guidebooks that have a daily reflection. Talk to God in your own words throughout the day, or sign up for a retreat. I am a priest in large part because of my parents' prayer lives. In the midst of raising six boys and working hard at their jobs, they both dedicated thirty minutes a day to prayer. The spiritual power of their relationship with God and their good example certainly rubbed off on us kids. When we get serious about prayer, the grace of our spiritual lives flows over like a fountain into the hearts and souls of those around us. Deepen your prayer life this year; if you find your days slipping away in busyness without any prayer time, start with five minutes of reflection and let your relationship with the Lord take you from there.

The second sign of a dynamic Catholic is ongoing formation in the faith. The 7 percent spend an average of fifteen minutes a day studying and learning about Catholicism, reading a good spiritual book, watching a video, or listening to a podcast or audiobook that deepens their understanding of some aspect of our beautiful teaching. Back in 1982, I took a computer class as an undergraduate at Marquette University—that is the extent of my technological training. Imagine me walking in to a company to apply for a computer job based on that! I would be laughed out of the building. Sadly, many Catholics stopped studying their faith in any meaningful way when they were confirmed. If our understanding of God and our religion stopped growing when we were teenagers, we will be tempted to reject it as a childish superstition or a nostalgic remnant of our early years. I always liken Catholicism to a five-thousand-room palace; if I'm lucky, I'll get into about twenty-five rooms in my lifetime. Our faith is so rich and deep. So, if you don't already do so, start reading some great books on the Catholic faith; your pastor would have some recommendations. Go online to the Vatican website or that of the United States Catholic Conference of Bishops. Watch Father Bob Barron's *Catholicism* series (available on his website, WordOnFire.org), or study the *Catechism of the Catholic Church*.

People frequently ask us Catholics questions about our faith. Why do you have to confess your sins to a priest? What's up with Purgatory? Why do you pray to the saints? Do you really believe the bread and wine become the Body and Blood of Christ? We all need to be intellectually equipped to give simple but substantive answers to such questions. If we cannot, we are missing precious opportunities to evangelize others. A friend of mine entered the Church when he finally met a Catholic who believed, practiced, and understood his faith. If we seek to be effective witnesses of the Crucified and Risen Christ, we need to be fueled by daily prayer and study or else our faith will become weak and ineffective.

The third sign is a remarkable generosity of spirit. Dynamic Catholics know that everybody and everything in their lives are gifts from God, meant to be cherished, shared, cultivated, and offered back to the Lord. The world may tell us that selfishness is the path to happiness, but we all know that the most joyful people are also the most generous ones. They have learned and absorbed the great secret paradox of the Gospel: if you seek life, you must lose yours; if you want to be first, go last; if you desire greatness, humble yourself; if you want to taste the Resurrection, embrace the Cross.

When I was in the Dominican Republic, I befriended a family that was even poorer than most. They had one of everything: one daughter, one table and chair, one bed and pot. They ate once a day and had one chicken. We always joked that we would have a big feast when that chicken was good and ready! One day, they got word to me that their daughter was sick, so I went bouncing up to their little house in the middle of nowhere in my sturdy truck, then anointed and blessed her; afterward, we sat outside, talking and watching a beautiful sunset and the emergence of a sea of stars. They made me sit on the chair since I was the guest; they sat on the ground.

When it was time to leave, the husband disappeared and came back with the chicken, offering it to me as a gift of gratitude for coming to anoint his daughter. I was overwhelmed by the offer and protested that he needed the chicken more than me; we argued for about ten minutes in Spanish until I realized he would be insulted if I refused such a magnanimous gift. So, there I was, going home in the pitch dark with a living, clucking chicken flapping around inside my truck.

I thought of the lesson of the widow's mite that appears in chapter 12 of the Gospel of Mark and in chapter 21 of Luke's Gospel—the two pennies a poor woman threw into the treasury box that represented her entire savings. Jesus praised the largesse of the sacrifice, the enormity of the gift. Dynamic Catholics are startlingly generous with their time, talent, and treasure because, like my Dominican friends, they live a profound gratitude and have mastered the great secret of Christ: if you want to find joy, peace, and fulfillment beyond your wildest dreams, make a sacrificial gift of your whole self for the sake of God and others. This deep truth is what Pope John Paul II, writing as Karol Wojtyła in his book *Love and Responsibility*, called "the law of the gift".

The fourth sign dynamic Catholics display is a deeply intuitive ability to evangelize others, witnessing their faith in Jesus to everyone around them. Known often as the "church lady" or the "religious guy" at work, seen as a spiritual leader and prayer warrior within their family, loved as the volunteers extraordinaire in their parishes, dynamic Catholics just instinctively share their faith. They read a great spiritual book and pass it on to a co-worker; they watch a Catholic video and share it with their daughter; they are not afraid to invite people to Mass or encourage someone to go to Confession. Because they are intent on growing in their understanding of the Catholic faith, they are able to articulate cogent, accurate, and substantive answers to spiritual questions.

Any good evangelical Christian is busy cultivating the faith of others, inviting people to attend Bible study, listening to their problems, praying with them, and bringing them to their church. For many generations, we Catholics have relied on a vibrant religious culture in families, parishes, and schools to form our people in the faith; in many ways, that culture has diminished, and so it is truly up to every single one of us to witness Jesus to others—this urgency fuels the energy of the New Evangelization. Every Catholic is called to be an effective evangelist and witness to the Crucified and Risen Jesus Christ.

Saint Teresa of Calcutta

On September 4, 2016, Pope Francis canonized Mother Teresa of Calcutta in the presence of hundreds of thousands of the faithful in St. Peter's Square.

How appropriate that Mother Teresa would be declared a saint in the Jubilee Year of Mercy. This short dynamic nun, who taught in an upper-class high school in India for many years before hearing the call to go live in the slums and serve the poorest of the poor, was a radiant icon of the mercy and love of Jesus Christ for the entire world. Her decision to leave her religious order and venture forth was met with many obstacles, doubts, and opposition, which required years of patience and prayer to overcome. Her fellow sisters thought she was too delicate for such a mission and would be back in a week. Mother Teresa was many things, but delicate and fearful she was not.

One of her first encounters in the streets was with a dying man, who was filthy, partially eaten by rats, and abandoned in a gutter. Mother tenderly picked him up, lovingly carried him to a local hospital for assistance, and patiently held him in her arms. At one point before he died, the woman looked at Mother Teresa with a question, "Why are you doing this?" In other words, why are you loving, helping, and touching me when no one else will? Her response was simple and beautiful, succinctly summarizing her spirituality of compassion. "Because I love you. Because I see Jesus in you."[1]

---

[1] *Mother Teresa*, produced by Ann and Jeanette Petrie (Petrie Productions, 1986).

This recognition, this "seeing" Jesus in the poor, abandoned, and suffering, enabled Mother Teresa to enter places
of disease, dirt, despair, poverty, and misery that most people would abhorrently avoid at all costs. She spent her entire
life and energy embracing this labor for the poor.

After her death, a priest who knew her well wrote an
account of Mother Teresa's life, focusing on her dark night
of the soul, her sense of being abandoned by God in the
midst of her ministry of compassion.[2] For decades, as she
traveled the globe serving the poor, she herself felt no consolation. In her prayer and heart, she felt God didn't love
her, that He wasn't listening, and that Heaven was closed
to her. She wondered if she would be saved, or if there was
really a Heaven at all. She shared these thoughts and feelings only within her spiritual journal, holding this inner
struggle within.

Imagine the paradox: this saintly sister, who brought
joy, love, and compassion to millions of suffering souls,
found no consolation at all in what she was doing. This
servant of mercy doubted if there was any mercy for her.

Yet, she never faltered. Unfailingly she arose at 4 A.M.
every morning to pray in the chapel in the dark, she went
about her heroic tasks as her order grew and expanded into
scores of countries in the most difficult and violent situations imaginable, and she always exuded tenderness, hope,
and confidence. Of such things are saints made.

At the beginning of her religious life, Mother Teresa
had asked for the grace to experience the fullness of what
Jesus had felt on the Cross. Was not the deepest part of
Christ's suffering His identification with our alienation
from God? In His cry from the Cross, "My God, my God,

---

[2] Brian Kolodiejchuk, M.C., *Mother Teresa: Come Be My Light; The Private
Writings of the Saint of Calcutta* (New York: Doubleday, 2007).

why have you forsaken me?"[3] Jesus feels, in His humanity, the consequence of our sin and death without ever having sinned Himself.

Pope Benedict XVI meaningfully states that, in this moment, it's as if God has turned against God.[4] Jesus' divine embrace of our broken humanity heals, forgives, and saves us. In requesting to share in the fullness of Jesus' Passion, Mother Teresa intensely lived that dark night of the soul. Like so many saints before her, she entered the crucible of the Paschal Mystery, making herself radically available to be used by God to heal and redeem the world—precisely through her own poverty, struggle, and suffering. Was it not Mother's own spiritual torment that allowed her to feel, live, and respond to the unspeakable sufferings of our brothers and sisters with a profound compassion seldom lived to such a profound depth? Our own wounded places become the blessed source of hope and healing for others when they are touched by the grace of Christ.

Mother Teresa was no poster-board saint who naïvely smiled at the mess of the world and blithely told people about the love of Jesus. She lived the Passion and death of the Lord in the darkest nights of her own soul and never gave up or broke down, sacrificing herself completely. She could look poverty, torment, and mortality fully in the face with joy because she knew the Christ of sleepless nights and unanswered questions, the One who awaits us within and on the other side of the distressing disguise.

---

[3] Mt 27:46; Jesus is quoting Ps 22:1.

[4] See Benedict XVI, Encylical Letter on Christian Love *Deus Caritas est* (December 25, 2005), no. 12, http://www.vatican.va/content/benedict-xvi/en /encyclicals/documents/hf_ben-xvi_enc_20051225_deus-caritas-est.html.

Stewardship: Give It Away

Discipleship, evangelization, and stewardship are all part of our unified response to the invitation of Christ to follow Him in faith, hope, and love. To cultivate a sense of stewardship in our lives is to ever more fully realize that everyone and everything in our lives is a gift from God.

In chapter 12 of John's Gospel, Jesus has dinner for the last time before His fearful Passion with His best friends in Bethany—Martha, Mary, and Lazarus. In the course of the evening, Mary breaks out an alabaster flask of genuine aromatic nard to anoint the feet of Jesus.

The Scriptures recount that the gift cost three hundred days' wages! Imagine spending a year's worth of salary to buy a gift for your best friend. This extravagant gesture shows a heart that is full of love, that does not count the cost, and that gives it all to express love for the Lord.

When we fall in love with God, we stop measuring what we give—the time spent in prayer and service, the financial gifts we make to the Church and to charity, the love and understanding we express, because we realize that all is a gift from the Lord, meant to be used for the building of the Kingdom.

The human tendency is to accumulate possessions, stuff, money, and Facebook friends as a cushion against insecurity, want, and fear. But we can never have enough of what we don't need, so we instinctively keep wanting more and more because it somehow makes us feel safer, more protected, and secure.

Jesus calls us to leave those desires behind and let Him be enough for us. This embrace of stewardship does not mean that we must live in a cardboard box, give all our money away, and leave our children in destitution. It does mean that we are sacrificially generous to the mission of the Kingdom when it comes to time, talent, and treasure, and we consciously strive to live with less in order to give more.

When we examine the lives of the saints, they clearly understood the Parable of the Pearl of Great Price in chapter 13 of Matthew's Gospel—the merchant who sells all he has in order to gain this precious jewel! In discovering the richness of the Lord's grace and love in our lives, earthly realities begin to pale in their attraction and importance to us. We can more readily trade material things for spiritual purposes because we realize that we are getting the better end of the bargain.

This discovery leads us to a life of gratitude where we can pass on, as a gift, what we ourselves received so gratuitously from the Lord of all gifts. The anointing at Bethany, Saint Francis of Assisi giving away all his possessions, Mother Teresa leaving the security of her convent, missionaries setting out for foreign lands and never returning—all of these heroic gestures evidence a radical response to the call of Christ. This attitude of gratitude translated into a life of generosity is the definition of stewardship.

I think of the thousands of remarkable servants who sacrificially give from their need to fuel the mission of the Church! Think of those in our parishes, schools, hospitals, charities, and services to the poor and sick who daily live out the Gospel. Most of these endeavors continue because of the radical donation of time, money, and love on the part of so many. A deep sense of stewardship already flourishes in the hearts of so many. The challenge is to grow this spirit in all of our people.

I always dream of what it would be like if every Catholic in the diocese celebrated the Eucharist every Sunday; prayed and read the Scripture every day; volunteered for one thing; put some donations in the collection basket; and evangelized the people in their lives. We would change the world even more than we are already doing.

Is such a vision just a naïve pipe dream? I don't think so.

Growing in faith is both a process and an event, where we pray, reflect, converse, and plan our future under the mighty power of the Holy Spirit. This whole experience will only be fruitful to the extent that it enables more and more of us to fall more deeply in love with God and the Church, to stake our lives on the power and truth of the Gospel, and to offer witness to the love and mercy of Christ.

Stewardship is how we live that out through deeds and actions as we offer the abundance of gifts we have received as a joyful oblation to the Lord.

A great quote I really like is, "Love is a basket with five loaves and two fish." It is never enough until you start to give it away.

Vocation to Holiness

In the past if someone was said "to have a vocation", the common understanding of this phrase was a religious calling to be a priest, sister, or brother. Even more than fifty years after Vatican II, we are still just beginning to grasp a fundamental Christian conviction rediscovered at the council: all members of the Church, by virtue of their baptisms, are called to holiness, to become saints, and to embrace their vocation in the world.

So, the question is not whether one has a vocation; it is, rather, what is my vocation? Whom and what is Christ calling me to embrace as my response to His presence and love in my life?

This universal call applies to us, in the sense that we are all invited to become disciples of the Lord Jesus and His holy Gospel and to become saints, daughters, and sons of the Father, transformed through grace to live as a new creation in this world.

Once we grow in this realization of our fundamental identity, we can then drill deeper and ask how we live out such a calling in the specificity of our own lives, with our talents and limitations, our desires and affections, our intellect and our strength? We need to continue to build a culture of vocation, where every single young person finds the necessary assistance to discern what the Lord is calling him to do.

Marriage and parenthood constitute a fundamental and holy vocation. Such a calling is a radical way to incarnate the love between Christ and the Church, to form a family built on faith, love, and self-giving. Marriage and family lie at the very heart of the Church's identity and mission.

Holy Orders and the consecrated life are particular ways of living out the radical call of the Gospel to be solely for the Lord and to dedicate everything to the up-building of the Church—God's holy people. The work of a vocations office and of religious orders is to build relationships with young people, to nurture that sense of divine call in them, and actively to seek candidates for the priesthood, permanent deaconate, and religious life.

This task, however, truly belongs to all of us, for we must all counsel, challenge, and support the young people of our communities to follow Christ and answer His call. The Lord continues to call us; the question is whether we can hear that gentle, yet persistent, voice in the noise and activity of our present culture. We need priests, religious, and deacons to carry on the preaching, teaching, sacramental life, and service to the world that has always characterized Catholicism.

In spiritual direction, many single people ask me if being single is a vocation in and of itself within the Church, or is it just a default because nothing else worked out? I consistently respond that it is a legitimate calling for millions of Catholics. Not every disciple is meant to be a priest, religious, or married. Singles live out the faith heroically, doing things not only explicitly within the Church, but also by their work in the world that builds up the Body of Christ. We need to support and welcome singles more effectively in our parishes and structures.

Lay ecclesial ministry has grown profoundly in the last fifty-plus years as a fruit of Vatican II. Catechists, directors of religious education, liturgists, teachers, parish directors, chaplains, nurses, and a plethora of other ministries have exploded in our parishes, as the laity take their rightful role as Christians co-responsible for the life and growth of the Church.

The challenge today is finding and supporting young people to embrace these important and responsible roles of service and leadership. The needed formation, the often low salaries, and the lack of recruitment stand as obstacles to the dynamic development of new lay leaders in our parishes and dioceses.

The Catholic faith has always lifted up the dignity and meaning of human work as a divine gift, as a way of participating in God's creation and redemption of the world. This conviction means that all labor that contributes to the common good is holy and, when done well and with a spiritual intention, can be an extraordinary way to sanctify the world. Whether one is a nurse, janitor, teacher, computer specialist, librarian, factory worker, or farmer, this particular career, this specific work, becomes an integral part of a personal vocation.

Within the Church, we will look at all these gifts and challenges regarding vocation, leadership, formation, and service. In the midst of so many fundamental paradigm shifts in our culture, how do we boldly hold up a life sacrificially and joyfully given to Christ as the path of human fulfillment and redemptive salvation, not only for ourselves but, indeed, for the whole world?

Our schools; parishes; religious education programs; priestly, diaconal, and lay ministry formation; parents; and families are all sacred places and persons entrusted with the task of building up a culture of vocation among everyone. This ecclesial task is *for* every member of the Church *by* every member of the Church. We hope and pray for a continued growth of service and mission.

Faithful Citizenship

From the dawn of the Church, Catholics have always sought to engage in the political process, to be good citizens, and to contribute to the common good. We do not separate ourselves from society, but rather, seek to be a leaven of Gospel and human values in order to build a culture of life and a civilization of love.

The Church calls us to form our consciences well, by embracing truth and goodness, by studying the Scriptures and the *Catechism of the Catholic Church*, in order to know the basic tenets of Catholic social teaching, to examine the facts of varying political choices, and to pray sincerely before voting. I offer this brief reflection, based on "Forming Consciences for Faithful Citizenship", the recently updated document published by the United States Conference of Catholic Bishops (USCCB) as a guide for us Catholics whenever we go to the polls.[1]

I quote paragraph 20 in its totality:

> The Church's teaching is clear that a good end does not justify an immoral means. As we all seek to advance the common good—by defending the inviolable sanctity of human life from the moment of conception until natural death, by promoting religious freedom, by defending marriage, by feeding the hungry and housing the

[1] The full title is "Forming Consciences for Faithful Citizenship, Part I—The U.S. Bishops' Reflection on Catholic Teaching and Political Life"; the entire document can be found on the USCCB's website.

homeless, by welcoming the immigrant and protecting the environment—it is important to recognize that not all possible courses of action are morally acceptable. We have a responsibility to discern carefully which public policies are morally sound. Catholics may choose different ways to respond to compelling social problems, but we cannot differ on our moral obligation to help build a more just and peaceful world through morally acceptable means, so that the weak and vulnerable are protected and human rights and dignity are defended.

The bishops' document applies Catholic teaching to major issues in Part II, outlining the fundamental threats to human life and dignity.[2] Abortion and euthanasia represent the direct killing of human life at its most vulnerable moments and must always be opposed. The bishops also condemn cloning and the destruction of human embryos, assisted suicide, genocide, torture, and the direct targeting of noncombatants in war or terrorist attacks. This fundamental right to life is the core of our social ethics and is also articulated in the Declaration of Independence.

Regarding capital punishment, quoting paragraph 67 in its entirety,

> Society has a duty to defend life against violence and to reach out to victims of crime. The Catholic Church has accepted the death penalty in the past for particularly egregious crimes when there was a serious continuing threat to society and no alternative was available. But our nation's continued reliance on the **death penalty** cannot be justified. Because we have other ways to protect society

[2] The full title is "Forming Consciences for Faithful Citizenship, Part II—Applying Catholic Teaching to Major Issues: A Summary of Policy Positions of the United States Conference of Catholic Bishops", which is also available on the USCCB's website.

that are more respectful of human life, the USCCB supports efforts to end the use of the death penalty and in the meantime to restrain its use through broader use of DNA evidence, access to effective counsel, and efforts to address unfairness and injustice related to application of the death penalty.

The Church tries to promote global peace among nations through her teaching and diplomacy. Countries have the right to defend the lives and safety of their citizens but are never justified in initiating hostilities. The Church has raised fundamental moral concerns about preventive use of military force, while honoring the commitment and sacrifice of our armed forces. We must work to reverse the spread of nuclear, chemical, and biological weapons. The bishops also support policies and actions that protect refugees of war and violence and all people suffering religious persecution throughout the world.

The Church is a strong supporter of marriage and family life, calling for policies that support marriage's traditional definition, as well as aiding families in their commitment and responsibility in the areas of taxes, divorce, immigration, and welfare. Living wages should allow workers to support their families with dignity. Children, in particular, should be valued, protected, and nurtured.

The bishops oppose contraceptive and abortion mandates in public programs and health plans that endanger rights of conscience. The document also upholds religious liberty as a fundamental human value and constitutional right, whereby no one may be forced to violate his moral conscience or religious beliefs.

The Church embraces a preferential option for the poor and economic justice, calling for a social order where all those who can work have the opportunity to do so with decent working conditions and just wages. The document affirms the right of workers to organize but also upholds economic freedom, initiative, and the right to private property. The Church calls for social programs and policies that will reduce poverty and increase self-sufficiency, stamp out hunger, and provide dignified housing for all people. Affordable and accessible health care is a fundamental human right.

"Faithful Citizenship" also calls for immigration policies that balance the Gospel call to welcome the stranger with the need for nations to control their borders and maintain the rule of law. The bishops affirm the right of parents to provide quality education for their children and the need to promote justice and stop violence, to combat discrimination, and to care for the environment. Global solidarity, especially with the millions of people who struggle to live in the developing world, is another priority. This essay is a brief commentary on the fundamental social and moral issues outlined in the bishops' document. I write it to encourage all of you to read "Forming Consciences for Faithful Citizenship" in its entirety before the next time that you vote, voting after you have read, studied, and prayed over the many challenges and issues that confront us as a world, nation, and local community.

Sadly, few, if any, political candidates embrace the totality of this coherent moral vision, as laid out in the bishops' document and the teachings of the Church; so we are called to exercise prudence and discernment as we weigh the platforms of parties and the positions of candidates. The sanctity of human life in all its challenges and forms, the dignity of the human person, and the need to build a world of love, justice, and mercy stand at the heart of the Catholic moral vision.

Part 3

God's Love Found in the Liturgical Year of the Church

Wait

We seem to live in a world of "instant everything". Fast food, social media, air travel, and thousands of conveniences designed to save time make us less willing to wait for anything. We now have instant Christmas, with holiday decorations in stores right after Halloween, Christmas music on the radio before Thanksgiving, and shopping opportunities at every turn.

While we can easily be drawn into the myriad of holiday activities right away, the Church offers us the season of Advent to help us prepare and wait for the gift of Christmas. And waiting is not necessarily a bad thing.

Great things can happen while we wait. A pregnant mother bonds with her unborn child for nine months while waiting for the birth. I've had great conversations with strangers in lines at stores and reception rooms of doctor's offices, which would never have happened if we didn't have to wait. The farmer waits for the right moment to plant and to harvest the fruits of the earth. Waiting compels us to pause, take a breath, and look around. When I am forced to wait, I am powerfully reminded that life doesn't revolve around me, my schedule, and my

This is a modified version of an article previously published as "Allow Advent to Be a Time of Silence, Prayer and Patience", *Northwest Indiana Catholic* (website), accessed September 15, 2020, https://www.nwicatholic.com/index .php/2011-10-28-15-52-16/bishop-hying-column?start=152.

needs. I am a small piece in a far larger plan and web of relationships. Waiting humbles us and helps us to find our proper place.

In the season of Advent, we listen to the voice of John the Baptist, who bids us to pay attention, to watch, and to prepare for the coming of the Messiah.[1] When I slow down, take the time truly to listen to someone, contemplate nature, read a book, and really pay attention, praying through my distractions, I begin to notice and sense the gentle presence of God in the smallest details of the remarkable life around me. How often we will suddenly notice a particular building, a picture on the wall, or another person in the hallway that we have passed dozens of times but never really saw, never took in, never paid attention to. Advent invites us to pace ourselves, not hurry up, to look, keep vigil, and listen with our hearts and spirits attuned to the in-breaking of the divine into the seemingly ordinary circumstances of life.

The Blessed Virgin Mary is the other spiritual figure that this season presents to us, this woman wrapped in silence, mystery, and grace. By embracing who God created her to be, Mary became the mother of Jesus, the sacred intersection point of the divine and the human.

Oftentimes, simply being ourselves is a difficult task. We can hide behind masks, walls, and indifference, fearing that if people truly knew the "real us", they wouldn't like what they see.

Advent is a sacred time to come before the Lord and let ourselves be seen by God, even as we try to slow down and see the divine presence around us. In prayer, I can drop my false self, the negative messages I play in my head, my worries and fears, all the baggage and agendas that

[1] See Mt 3; Mk 1; Lk 3; Jn 1.

sometimes rob me of joy and peace, and just be myself, the real me that God loves and takes delight in.

Prayer is a taste of the ecstasy of Heaven because it calls me to live radically in the present moment. Distractions will try to pull me into the future or the past, but when I can keep returning to the sacred experience of now, I find the Lord in all of the beauty, truth, and goodness of the divine visitation. Prayer is the most human and liberating experience that we can embrace.

Wouldn't it be odd if we celebrated our best friend's birthday, but got so distracted by the party, gifts, decorations, and cooking that we never actually sat down and talked to the person we are trying to honor? The best present is presence. Maybe during Advent, God is calling you to forgo some of the frenzy—do less shopping and pray more; attend fewer holiday events and do more volunteer service; run around less and spend more time just being, watching, and waiting along with Mary, John the Baptist, all the saints, and the entire Church for the surprising revelation of Jesus—His presence, love, mercy, and life.

My prayer for Advent (and I admit it is a strange one!) is that life will force us to wait sometimes, to not get everything we want right away, and to be compelled to anticipate, so that we will stop, look, and listen in new ways. Let Advent be a time of silence, prayer, and patience as the Lord secretly works in the corners of our hearts, helping us to carry and birth the living Christ for this hurting world.

The Kindness of Saint Nicholas

December 6 is the traditional Feast of Saint Nicholas. Serving as a bishop in what is now Turkey in the fourth century, Nicholas was renowned for his love and generosity toward the poor, often secretly leaving food, clothing, and gifts at people's doors in the middle of the night. This generous practice of kindness made him the great inspiration for Santa Claus. His feast is a warm-up for Christmas, as children who leave shoes or stockings out the night before will find them filled with gifts and goodies in the morning.

Nicholas inspires me to reflect on kindness—the basic love, goodness, and generosity that eases suffering, sadness, and loneliness, the thoughtful gesture that can turn a so-so day into a delight. There can never be enough kindness in the world, and a little bit of it can go a long way toward brightening the life of another person. Here are some things that I try to work on consistently (and fail at regularly) to thread more kindness into my relationships with others.

Be gentle. In a world that is sometimes harsh and cold, a gentle word, a note of thanks, a caustic comment withheld, patient listening, all can transform the life of another.

This is a modified version of an article previously published as "In the Spirit of St. Nicholas, Generously Practice Love and Kindness", *Northwest Indiana Catholic* (website), accessed September 15, 2020, https://www.nwicatholic.com/index.php/2011-10-28-15-52-16/bishop-hying-column?start=151.

Oftentimes, we take out our anger and stress on the people that least deserve it—our family. Cutting remarks and angry comments can be apologized for but not always erased from the memories and hearts of the people around us. Sometimes, it's easier to be kinder to strangers than our relatives or co-workers. Gentleness reflects the peace and joy of the Lord.

Give the benefit of the doubt. I can easily rush to judgment without knowing all the facts and often put a negative interpretation on the actions of another without fully understanding the situation. Presuming goodwill and proper intentions saves me from slandering, misjudging, and gossiping about others.

How much more understanding would I be if I completely knew the real story of another person's difficulties and crosses? As the saying goes, "Be kind to everyone you meet because they are all fighting a hard battle."

Go the extra mile. When I am trying to accomplish my tasks and agenda, the needs and requests of others can feel like intrusions and obstacles. I try to see the interruptions as my real work—taking the time to really listen to someone who has a problem, making that extra pastoral visit, calling someone who is grieving; these are the little things that often make a world of difference to another person. We can never know how one kind gesture or word will transform the life of someone, giving him hope and courage to go on. There is no love without sacrifice.

Stop complaining. No one is attracted to crabbiness. No one looks at a complaining, negative, griping person and says, "I want more of that in my life!" There is certainly a lot to be sad and negative about in the world—for example, poverty, malnutrition, violence, terrorism, abortion, abused children, and despair—but giving in to hopelessness only increases the darkness. We may carry some heavy crosses, and life will break our hearts, but the good always outweighs the bad. My gratitude list is always longer than my complaint sheet. Joyful hope and a positive spirit buoy the lives of those around us. We need to each ask ourselves, "Are people happier, more hopeful, and more at peace because they encountered me today?"

Help the poor. An integral component of the Gospel is to love and serve the poor in the name of Christ. The Church holds up both charity and justice, calling us to serve the immediate needs of those who are trapped in poverty and suffering, but also to advocate for the needed social transformation that attacks poverty at its roots. As Nicholas and so many of the saints discovered, Jesus comes to us in the distressing disguise of the poor. To love and serve someone in need with friendship, time, attention, money, and food is to touch Christ Himself.

While we work for a just and equitable social order, we help the people who fall between the economic cracks now, so that they have the necessities to live a dignified and human life. Many years ago, my family decided to stop giving gifts to each other for Christmas; everybody has everything he could possibly need or want. We give the money to charities instead to benefit those with the least. Wouldn't this be a great year to break with some of the consumerism that surrounds us and keep Christmas simple?

When I was the rector of a seminary, I would often exhort the seminarians simply to be kind to people, to be flexible on the things that can be adjusted, to lift others up, and to be gently merciful. "You may not be another Fulton Sheen in the pulpit or the greatest administrator, but if you are simply kind and loving to your people and do your best, you will be a faithful and effective pastor," I would say. What I encouraged our future priests to embrace can apply to all of us.

As Saint Peter says, "Love covers a multitude of sins."[1] And in First Corinthians, Saint Paul reminds us that we can do the greatest things imaginable, but if we act without love in our hearts, none of it matters.[2] Advent and Christmas are all about Love coming to our rescue and saving us from sin and death. Love never fails.

[1] 1 Pet 4:8.
[2] 1 Cor 13:1–3.

What Is Joy?

The third Sunday of Advent is traditionally called Gaudete Sunday; *gaudete* means "let us rejoice" in Latin. We light the rose candle on this day to mark the fact that we are now closer to Christmas than the beginning of Advent. Jesus is near, and so we rejoice! In our world that is often marked by fear, darkness, and sadness, we Christians are called to be prophetically joyful.

What is joy, and how do we get more of it in our lives? Sometimes, life just feels too heavy and the burdens too great for us to be light in spirit and hopeful about the future of the world. But faith roots us in a destiny and purpose far greater than we can imagine. Understanding and embracing joy helps us through the dark nights of life. When I contrast joy with pleasure, satisfaction, and happiness, it helps toward a greater understanding.

Eating a favorite food, sleeping in on a Saturday morning, going on vacation, or buying a new smartphone may give us pleasure. Our senses take in pleasure, and we enjoy the sensation in the moment. Pleasure is fun, but it does not last. My favorite dessert gives me pleasure while

This is a modified version of an article previously published as "Rooted in the Love of the Lord, No Suffering, Setback, Sadness Can Rob Us of Joy", *Northwest Indiana Catholic* (website), accessed September 15, 2020, https://www.nwi catholic.com/index.php/2011-10-28-15-52-16/bishop-hying-column?start =150.

I am eating it, but the delight of the experience lasts no longer than the last bite. So, there has to be more to life than just pleasure.

Working out at the gym is deeply satisfying, but not necessarily pleasurable. Doing things that are healthy and life-giving, both for ourselves and others, can be fulfilling way beyond what pleasure offers. Hours after I have worked out or accomplished some task, I still feel good about it and feel some positive effects, but satisfaction doesn't necessarily lift the banners or blow the trumpets. Satisfaction alone does not nourish the heart or the spirit, so maybe we are really looking for happiness.

Marrying the right person, working a dream career, enjoying good health, and being surrounded by family and friends can bring us great happiness, a deep sense of elation way beyond fleeting moments of pleasure or passing hours of satisfaction. We all want to be happy in our relationships and our work. But, as we painfully know, loved ones pass away, health declines, and jobs are sometimes lost; the people and situations that we pinned our happiness on disappear and we suddenly feel lost, disoriented, and betrayed by life. So there has to be something even deeper than happiness that goes to the very core of who we are. That mysterious reality is joy!

Back in 1992, my brother Will was working in Jamaica, building houses for the homeless in Kingston. His organization ran out of money, so I did a fundraiser in the parish where I served to continue the good work. Bearing a big check and a video camera, I went to visit my brother and film the fruit of our parishioners' remarkable generosity. While in Jamaica, I visited and celebrated Mass at a home for lepers, served by a group of religious sisters.

I had never met a leper before, so I was a little nervous going in, not knowing what to expect. I encountered people who had lost fingers and toes, arms, and legs; the disease had consumed the faces of some residents, leaving them terribly disfigured and scarred. What I remember most vividly nearly thirty years later, however, is not the missing body parts of the residents, but rather their incredible, inexplicable joy! I am not sure if I have ever encountered a group of people either before or since that were so absolutely, riotously joyful. Their smiles, laughter, and lively conversation filled the residence with a radical, infectious joy.

When we know that we are loved by God, when we have encountered His tender mercy, when we realize our deepest identity as beloved children of the Father, we experience the joy of the Kingdom of Heaven. No suffering, setback, or sadness can rob us of joy if we stay rooted in the love of the Lord. We may lose all pleasure, satisfaction, and happiness, but no one and nothing can take away our joy without our permission.

This fundamental truth I learned from the beautiful folks with leprosy and so many others in similar situations of suffering and difficulty. When we are tempted to let life rob us of peace and joy, we need to focus on the truth and meaning of Advent and Christmas: God coming to us in the poverty of our human condition; Jesus embracing everything within us that was lost, dark, and dead; the Lord opening us to mercy, forgiveness, and eternal life.

We know how the story of our lives and the history of the world will end; we have the book of Revelation. God, life, love, and joy win out over the forces of sin and death. When we know who we are and where we are going, life becomes joyful for us. As Saint Catherine of Siena said, "All the way to heaven is heaven because Christ is the Way."[1]

---

[1] Regis Martin, *The Last Things: Death, Judgment, Heaven, Hell* (San Francisco: Calif.: Ignatius Press, 1998), p. 39.

The Satisfaction of Preparing for the Kingdom

During my first assignment as an associate pastor at St. Anthony Parish in Menomonee Falls, Wisconsin, where about ninety weddings took place every year, I was always busy doing marriage preparation with engaged couples essentially my own age. I loved it!

The biggest challenge was helping them to see beyond the excitement and immediacy of the wedding plans and prepare for a lifelong sacramental marriage in the Church. Invitations, flowers, the dinner, and the reception matter, but building a shared life in Christ is the true heart of marriage preparation.

Advent is a lot like working with engaged couples. Yes, we prepare for Christmas, buying gifts, throwing parties, and sending out greeting cards. But the Scripture readings for this season call us to a broader vision of the meaning of Christ's birth, inviting us to simultaneously look backwards, forwards, and around us. We look back to the historical birth of the Lord Jesus two thousand years ago

This is a modified version of an article originally published as "Advent Calls Us to Realization That God Breaks into Our Lives at Any Given Moment", *Northwest Indiana Catholic* (website), November 27, 2016, https://www.nwicatholic.com/index.php/2011-10-28-15-52-16/bishop-hying-column/4036-advent-calls-us-to-realization-that-god-breaks-into-our-lives-at-any-given-moment.

as a most significant moment when God entered into our world as a human being to save us from sin and death.

This Word-made-Flesh, this Incarnation of the Son of God, changed everything, uniting us in the most intimate way with the Lord, opening the way to the Kingdom of God, to redemption, mercy, and forgiveness. The Church never stops inviting us to look back to the beginning of Christianity, to the tenderness, humility, love, and goodness of the Christ.

The Gospel for the first Sunday of Advent always speaks about the end of the world, which seems a little jarring. Aren't we cozily focusing on the Babe of Bethlehem, not cataclysmic events that will mark the Apocalypse?

In this scriptural proclamation, we are to look forward, reminded that Advent is about not only what occurred long ago but also what will happen in the future. Just as Jesus established the reign of God two thousand years ago, so too He will return at the end of time to usher in its fulfillment. We live in this in-between time, confident that our efforts to love, serve, and pray, as well as our efforts to offer mercy and forgiveness and to work for justice and goodness, make an invaluable contribution to the final form of God's Kingdom—yet knowing that our human efforts alone are never enough.

God's grace, mercy, and power will triumph over the forces of sin and death forever. This final coming of Christ brings to completion His first one.

Advent also invites us to look around in the immediacy of the present moment and to recognize the hour of the divine visitation, knowing that God is breaking into our lives on a regular basis if we have the eyes to see and the ears to hear.

What action, attitude, change of heart, risk, or surrender is the Lord inviting you to embrace this Advent? We could probably all benefit from more silence, less noise, more peace, less frenzy, more service of the needy, less superfluous shopping, more attention to Scripture, and less time on the computer or television. In between the first and the second comings of Christ is the constant Advent of the now, the present moment, the immediacy of the situation, events, responsibilities, and people I find myself immersed in.

Both in Milwaukee and in Northwest Indiana, I love walking along Lake Michigan, especially at dusk, watching the sunset, observing the emergence of the moon and stars, feeling the healing calm of the waves, and viewing the blue horizon over the water. I look up at the heavens and realize that somewhere beyond the stars, beyond space and time, is the mysterious Kingdom of Heaven, our ultimate destiny and home, a relationship with God and others that has already begun but is not yet accomplished—a divine banquet where all human hunger and longing is satisfied, where infinite love will triumph forever, and where the Wedding Feast of the Lamb will go on perpetually.

Just as I once sat for endless hours with hundreds of engaged couples all those years ago, inviting them to look beyond the immediacy of invitation lists, menu choices, and dress colors to prepare for a lifetime of marital joy, communion, and love in Christ, so too, during Advent, God beckons us to sit with Him; to lay aside momentarily the shopping lists, party preparations, and decorating plans, so that we can listen to the divine voice speaking in the silence; to remove the obstacles that keep us from being free and happy; to envision the Kingdom of God in all of its glory; to ponder the vulnerability and humility of the Christ Child; and to prepare ourselves for the Marriage Feast to come.

Planning a wedding or preparing for Christmas may seem more urgent, but building a marriage or preparing for the Kingdom is ultimately more satisfying! Advent should always be joyful, peaceful, and prayerful. Don't let all the busyness keep you too occupied to seek the Lord. He is looking for us!

The Christmas Dance

The holy, joyful, and grace-filled season of Christmas fills us with hope, reminding us that our relationships with God and each other matter more than anything else. We hope to know and deeply feel the extraordinary love of God in our lives.

As we celebrate the joyous feast of Christmas, the tender mercy of God never fails to move our hearts! God truly has compassion for all the limits, difficulties, sufferings, and setbacks of our human condition, so much so that He became human Himself, accepting the totality of our experience with the only exception of sin. God enters the world, unbidden and unnoticed, born as a fragile child on the fringes of the Roman Empire to poor parents, who "laid him in a manger, because there was no place for them at the inn".[1] Mercy is the name for this "love coming to the rescue" of our sin and death.

We pray for the grace to experience the love of the Lord in ever deeper and transformative ways, through the Word of God; the sacraments, especially the Eucharist and Reconciliation; service to the poor and sick; and loving those around us with tender concern. Is this the "kairos" moment to mend a friendship, offer an apology, look at someone we often judge with new eyes, visit the lonely,

[1] Lk 2:7.

147

give the Church another chance, and open our hearts to God's gentle presence?

As the world seems to fall into greater violence, fear, and chaos, are we not called to bear the Light of God—Jesus Christ—to others, even as that Light has shone within our own hearts?

I often reflect in prayer on the fact that there was no room in the inn for the Holy Family when the time came for the birth of the Son of God. In our lives of busyness, distraction, clutter, and stuff, in this world of suffering, violence, conflict, and despair, often it feels that there is little room for peace, justice, mercy, and love, little space for God to take up residence, come in, sit, and love us. Yet, unbidden and often unnoticed, Jesus shows up anyway, inviting us into that sacred space within ourselves where heart speaks to heart, calling us to share the Eucharist and the Gospel with each other, bidding us to live the dream of the Kingdom of God in the here and now.

At Christmas, we celebrate the startling truth that the eternal, invisible, and powerful God humbled Himself to embrace our humanity, becoming visible, vulnerable, and available to each of us. In the whole Christ event, God seeks us out to save and redeem what was lost and broken. He visited our planet two thousand years ago and fell so in love with us that He chose to stay! Through the Church and her sacraments, in prayer and service, in relationship and love, Jesus Christ draws near to us and abides in our lives and communities through the wonder of divine grace. This conviction should make us get up and dance!

CHRISTMAS

Peace Is a Person

Whenever anyone asks me what I want for Christmas, I always say, "World peace." The questioner usually does not find that response particularly helpful, but it is my sincere and true answer. We live in a world torn apart by violence—the destruction of war, the evil of terrorism, the nightmare of Syria, the martyrdom of Christians, the shootings in our streets, and abuse of people beyond reckoning. Add to that sad narrative the violence of words and attitudes against minorities, women, the unborn, the poor, and just about every other group of people imaginable.

We call Jesus Christ the Prince of Peace, the One whose coming in the flesh has ushered in the Kingdom of God and whose vision invites us to dream and build a civilization of love, respect, justice, mercy, and truth. When our hearts and lives take root in the life of God, true peace will flourish because we will genuinely love everyone and seek the common good. So much violence flows from the disorder of injustice, hatred, indifference, greed, and abuse. As Pope Paul VI famously said in his 1972 World Day of Peace message, "If you want peace, work for justice."

This is a modified version of an article originally published as "A Christmas Message from Bishop Donald J. Hying", *Northwest Indiana Catholic* (website), December 18, 2016, https://www.nwicatholic.com/index.php/2011-10-28-15-52-16/bishop-hying-column?start=107.

As we contemplate the peacefulness of the Nativity scene, we can feel the love shared between Joseph and Mary, for God, each other, and the Christ Child. We see this warm, vulnerable, little baby—God come in the Flesh, come to love, heal, bless, and forgive.

Just beyond the immediacy of that beautiful Christmas scene, however, lies the poverty of the Holy Family, the murderous jealousy of King Herod, the shadow of Roman persecution and rejection, and the mystery of the Cross. This paradoxical mixture of light and darkness, peace and violence, love and hate, acceptance and rejection, teaches us that we can actually attain true peace in this life only if we stay centered in the love of the Lord, despite the swirl of conflict all around us. God calls us to loving, just, merciful, and joyous relationships.

May we become ever more effective peacemakers, bridge builders who offer hearts of love and mercy to everyone around us, especially those who are broken, sad, angry, and marginalized.

The world needs peace more than ever. We know the secret answer of how to achieve it. Peace is a Person, not just an experience, and when we live in the love of God, peace breaks out all over the place. During the Christmas season, may the Prince of Peace fill your minds and hearts with goodness and joy!

LENT

The Strangest Thing

During Holy Week, the strangest thing occurs. Millions of Christians throughout the world gather to honor the humiliation, torture, and Crucifixion of Jesus Christ. In a global culture that usually celebrates power, strength, and beauty, this public reverence of something so horrific is always a little shocking. Could it be that what so many people find absolutely compelling about the Passion narrative is the vulnerability of God?

In the Christ event, God leaves the safety and glory of Heaven, in a sense, and embraces the limitations of our human condition, coming to know in the flesh both the glory and the tragedy of our nature without ever sinning. In the last week of His life, Jesus completely hands Himself over to us. In the foot washing and the Eucharist, in the scourging and the Crucifixion, the Son of God loves us completely, without restrictions, conditions, or limits. Whether we accept, reject, or ignore this Divine Love, Jesus does not change His stance toward us.

In Roman and Greek mythology, the gods are always scheming to manipulate humanity to serve their often selfish ends and ego-driven schemes. In Christ, we encounter

This is a modified version of an article originally published as "Holy Week: Celebrating the Strangest Things", *Catholic Herald*, March 28, 2013, https://catholicherald.org/catholic-herald/general/holy-week-celebrating-the-strangest-things/.

the startling subversion of this oppressive game. God serves us! In total humility, availability, vulnerability, and mercy, God has come to love, forgive, and save us. The weakness of the Cross, the simplicity of the Eucharist, the shock of the foot washing, the love that seeks to embrace a traitor, a thief, and a coward, is so far beyond the competition of power politics, the whirl of social hubris, and the grasp of worldly striving that it takes our breath away. No wonder kings will stand speechless in the presence of the Suffering Servant, as the prophet Isaiah proclaims in his biblical account.

If God could become that poor, vulnerable, and humble to love me, then how can I ever stand on my self-importance? During Holy Week we celebrate the strangest things—weakness becomes strength, love conquers fear, wretched despair gives way to resurrected hope, and never-ending death is swallowed up by eternal life—and it is all because a naked criminal was thrown down on a cross two thousand years ago and He embraced it as if it were His marriage bed.

Jesus' Incarnation, fasting in the wilderness, miracles of healing and forgiveness, nights spent in prayer, horrific death, and glorious rising are all for you and me. To contemplate the enormity of God's love for us is already to feel in our pulse and flesh the eternal beat of the Resurrection.

LENT

What Lent Is All About

Lent is always a graced period for us, as the Church invites us to go into a forty-day retreat in the desert with the Lord and all of those preparing to celebrate the Easter sacraments.

Oftentimes, we give up something for Lent as a form of penance—chocolate, television, and snacking. I usually give up coffee but always do it cold turkey. Two days after Ash Wednesday, I'm ready to check into the hospital for caffeine withdrawal, but then it gets better. Some year I hope to do it smarter. Does God really care if we sacrifice something, embrace a penance, or fast regularly?

In a discussion with the Pharisees about why His disciples do not fast, Jesus reshapes the practice of fasting as a sign of our incompleteness, our longing for the fullness of God's Kingdom, and the presence of the Messiah.[1]

When we feel depressed, anxious, lonely, or needy, we all get the urge to fill that longing with a quick fix. Alcohol, shopping, food, or television become ways to fill the hole in our hearts, to relieve what we are feeling within, and to take our mind off the emptiness. Fasting of any kind becomes a sacred reminder that only God can fulfill our

This is a modified version of an article originally published as "Consider How the Forty Days of Lent Can Become a Spiritual 'Game-Changer'", *Northwest Indiana Catholic* (website), January 31, 2016, https://www.nwicatholic.com/index.php/2011-10-28-15-52-16/bishop-hying-column?start=145.

[1] See Mt 9; Mk 2; Lk 5.

deepest desires. I can live without coffee, snacks, cigarettes, cable news, and beer, but I can't survive without prayer, love, and mercy. I can't take my next breath without the Holy Spirit. I can't hope for eternal life without Jesus.

Fasting and penance remind me that I am just passing through this world—that I can't afford to cling to anything, except the Lord. Voluntarily renouncing some of the pleasures of this life orients me toward the good things of the Kingdom. Fasting reminds me that we are not fully there yet, but are well on the way.

Lent also focuses on almsgiving, reaching out to those in need with greater generosity and compassion. The Lord calls us to encounter the suffering and the poor with greater intention and feeling. What will we do?

I try to go somewhere every week of Lent, whether it's a meal program, a hospital, a nursing home, or a homeless shelter, to seek out God's beautiful children. It's not so much that I have anything to give that will help them, transform their lives, or change their situations. I hear God calling me to go because I am in need of help, transformation, and conversion. A visit with the poor and suffering is a 100 percent guaranteed encounter with the living Christ.

In light of the Lord's mercy, I have reflected and prayed more profoundly on how tender and compassionate God is with me, despite all of my sins and errors, and how I am called to be that merciful face of the Lord to others. The Lord's Prayer reminds us that we can only receive the gift of God's forgiveness to the extent that we are willing to pass on what none of us deserve, but all of us long for and need. Who needs to feel your love, mercy, kindness, and concern? Ask the Lord each morning to use you to be His tenderness to others.

How painful yet joyous is it to grapple with our own betrayals and harshness, to embrace our weakness, to lift it to the Lord in Reconciliation, and then to be freed of the debt, the guilt, and the burden. In that newfound freedom, we can help lift the heavy weight that others carry around.

I have come to realize over and over again that the greatest thing I can do for others is to pray, to offer the Eucharist, to spend time in Eucharistic Adoration, to meditate on Scripture, to be faithful to the Liturgy of the Hours, and to lift up the many needs of the people I serve. As Christians, all of our activity flows to and from our relationship with the Lord.

Lent is a great time to enter more deeply into prayer, to find a practice and a routine that will draw us into daily conversation and time spent with God. If we are not actively and intentionally developing our prayer life, we will never become the intimate friend of the Lord that He longs us to be. Our discipleship will never be fully fruitful. We will miss out to some extent on our fundamental purpose.

My best prayer times are when I am on retreat at a Trappist monastery—the monks chanting the psalms in the early morning dark, the silence that is so deep as to be an inner voice of peace, the solitude that knocks out all distractions. I can pray there as naturally as breathing. God is so real, I can touch Him! Then I come back to the work, stresses, and schedules of "real" life and my prayerful centeredness vanishes like a wisp of smoke. I know the challenge is to build the monastery in my heart, to seek the stillness in the midst of the noise, to seek out those places and times of prayer that beckon even in the midst of overflowing schedules.

Fasting, prayer, and almsgiving is what Lent has always been about.

The Balance of Yes and No

The liturgy for the first Sunday of Lent always proclaims the Gospel of Jesus' temptation in the wilderness, found in chapter 4 of both Matthew's Gospel and Luke's. While spending forty days in the desert, fasting and praying at the beginning of His ministry, the Lord is tempted by Satan to use His divine powers for Himself instead of the service and salvation of others. We hear Jesus emphatically say no three times to the tempter, as He says yes to the will of the Father.

Every day, each of us is faced with hundreds of decisions to which we must either say yes or no. Sometimes, the choice is clear if not necessarily easy; we know what is good and what is bad for us and other people. Should I eat fast food or cook a healthy meal? Other times, the decision is ambiguous because it is a choice between two goods. Should I help out at the parish fish fry or spend time with my grandchildren? We are invited to contribute to so many causes, volunteer for another great event, and help just one more person. We live in a world of infinite opportunity and need but only have limited time, energy, and resources.

This is a modified version of an article originally published as "Questions to Ponder as We Enter into the Forty Days of Lent", *Northwest Indiana Catholic* (website), February 7, 2016, https://www.nwicatholic.com/index.php/2011-10 -28-15-52-16/bishop-hying-column?start=144.

I attended a bishops' leadership training entitled "Balancing the Demands of Ministry and Living Your Vocation", sponsored by the Catholic Leadership Institute. Practical and concrete, the seminar taught me the importance of setting priorities, managing time and schedules, and the need to say no to many things in order to ensure time and energy for the essential tasks.

Like many of you, I want to say yes to everything that people ask me to do, to be present, responsive, and helpful when I can, but when we acquiesce to everything, we will soon feel overwhelmed, stressed, and exhausted.

During the seminar, we watched a video presentation by Bishop George Niederauer, the Archbishop Emeritus of San Francisco, who spoke very powerfully about all the times Jesus said no to legitimate and reasonable requests in order to give a fuller yes to the Father's will. I quote it at length because it is so helpful to look at Jesus' ministry in this way.

> Jesus did say no and not only to Satan three times in the desert. Jesus said no or its equivalent when a yes did not fit in with His yes to the Father. The instances are many.... Let me bury my father before I follow you: NO (Mt 8); tell my sister to help me with the housework: NO (Lk 10); tell my brother to be fair with me about our inheritance: NO (Lk 12); stay in our town a little longer: NO (Lk 4); to the cured Gerasene demoniac let me follow you: NO (Mk 5).

> Close, loving friends, with apparently the strongest personal claims on Him, also asked favors: give my sons a special privileged place next to you: NO (Mk 10); stop talking about your death like that: NO (Mk 8); tell us when the last things will occur: NO (Acts 1); call down fire from Heaven to destroy those that reject you: NO (Lk 9).

Also, there were demands of the crowds: work a sign for us right here and now: NO (Mt 12); do here in your own town the things we have heard you did in Capernaum: NO (Lk 4); give us again today the bread you gave us yesterday: NO (Jn 6).

Finally, Jesus received many common sense kinds of requests: send the crowds away, they're getting hungry: NO (Lk 9); keep this crowd quiet: NO (Lk 19); make your followers fast like those of John the Baptizer: NO (Mk 2); surely you have some answer to these accusations against you: NO (Mk 15). Jesus said no whenever He had to do so in order to continue His lifelong yes to His Father's loving, saving will.

In many ways, we are programmed as Christians to say yes to everything that people ask us to do, and may feel guilty when we say no, but we know deep-down that a constant yes is impossible to sustain. So, the challenge is to discern God's will in our lives by looking at our relationships and responsibilities, to listen to the voice of God in our prayer, and to respond as generously as we can to new and unexpected situations of need and service, but not at the expense of our fundamental commitments and priorities.

For example, it would be wrong to spend so much time volunteering at the parish that I am never home with my family or to spend so much time working that I never have time to pray or rest. Learning to balance competing goods is a difficult but necessary skill for the Christian disciple as it was for Jesus.

During Lent, I want to become more aware of what I say yes and no to. Where am I dissipating my time and energy that keeps me scattered and unfocused? What activities do I need to say no to in order to say yes to more prayer, reflection, and rest? What negative attitudes or thoughts do I need to reject in order to embrace the joy, peace, and love of the Lord more fully? What do I need to discard and give away in order to live with more focus, simplicity, and energy? What inner cravings for attention, control, and comfort need to be put aside so that there is more room for the action of the Holy Spirit?

These questions must be the ones that Jesus wrestled with in the wilderness, fresh from His Baptism, poised to begin His public ministry. They are worthy questions for us as well as we enter into the desert for the forty days of Lent with the Lord at our side.

Dethrone the False Self

Jesus experiences the temptations of Satan in the wilderness as the Evil One attempts to derail the purpose and focus of Jesus' life and ministry by tempting Him to use His divine powers and extraordinary gifts for Himself, instead of the liberation and salvation of the human race. Clearly, much is at stake in this battle of wills, as the Lord stands poised to begin His astonishing public ministry of healing, forgiving, teaching, and casting out demons.

We may think that the temptation in the wilderness was an easy one for Jesus to resist. After all, He is the Son of God, a divine person, sinless, and holy. Yet, the Lord was also fully human and struggled with temptations, just as we do. This truth is deeply consoling for it signifies that Jesus fully understands our weakness, fragility, and inconsistency. He comes to our rescue as God but fully identifies with our humanity in all of its ambiguity and complexity.

This temptation scene in the desert teaches us that if we disconnect power from the love and service of others, it rapidly becomes selfish, destructive, and even demonic. How many political leaders and governments have killed millions of people, trampled on human rights, and strangled the common good because they used power for their own selfish and destructive ambitions? How many economic systems and corporations have pursued raw profit as the only value, as in the case of unfettered capitalism or the virtual enslavement of the worker to the service of the state, as in the case of Marxism?

Such structures dehumanize people in order to idolize things. In the Dominican Republic, I saw firsthand how the sugarcane companies held Haitian workers in horrible living conditions, brutal physical labor, and indentured servitude in order to produce cheap sugar that was still profitable for the owners. Power unharnessed from love becomes destructive.

We can observe this same phenomenon in the Church. Clericalism can make some members of the clergy arrogant and self-centered; in such cases, the focus of ministry becomes the cleric's comfort, authority, and agenda, instead of the pastoral care of God's people. Ecclesial ministers, both lay and clergy, can engage in turf wars, in conflict and competition with each other, instead of working as a team for the spreading of the Gospel. Parish volunteers can become so possessive of the work they do that no new people or ideas can ever penetrate the walls they have built. We only need to read Paul's epistles to realize that all such negative behavior and attitudes are as old as the foundation of the Church, but they remain antithetical to Christ and His Gospel.

All of us, in our experiences of work, school, family, Church, and friendships, have probably suffered at the hands of another because of the fundamental misuse of power, whether that power be physical, psychological, economic, spiritual, or structural. Such painful situations can either embitter us or convert us. We can either exact some sort of revenge when we gain power ourselves or we can break the cycle of abusive fear by embracing Jesus' example.

Christ intimately knew God the Father and the secrets of Heaven; He could raise the dead, multiply food, calm storms, heal physical maladies, perform exorcisms, and

forgive sins. If anyone in the entire breadth of human history would have had a right to be proud and arrogant, it
would have been Jesus. But we see just the opposite.

As Saint Paul proclaimed, "Though he was in the form
of God, [he] did not deem equality with God a thing to be
grasped, but emptied himself, taking the form of a servant,
being born in the likeness of men."[1]

Jesus understood well that true power must always serve
the needs of others in love and humility, and that we are
only entrusted with talents, gifts, authority, knowledge,
and wealth so that we can become servant leaders who
bring others to the fullness of their human potential by our
own witness to holiness, love, humility, and service.

In my priestly ministry, I have always called both
engaged couples and seminarians (and hopefully myself) to
grow in self-knowledge and humility, to develop enough
of an integrated self, so that they can give themselves fully
to their spouses, whether that be a husband, a wife, or the
Church. Otherwise, we enter into our vocations, not asking what I can give, but rather, what I can get, not how
can I serve, but rather, how I can get others to serve me.

Without humility, we subtly organize our lives with
ourselves enthroned at the center. Power unchained from
self-emptying love invariably damages others and us.

Lent is an opportune time to dethrone the false self, the
persona that craves attention, control, power, and possessions. Fasting, prayer, and almsgiving teach us that God is
the center of everything, including our hearts. When we
let God be God for us, everything moves in a beautiful
harmony around that sacred center. Lent is a moment to
let the Lord empty us out, so that what remains is His
abiding and radiant presence. In the desert, Jesus had nothing except His Father, so actually He had everything.

[1] Phil 2:6–7.

Touch the Wounds

In the summer of 1987, as part of my seminary training, I did a hospital chaplaincy internship in New Orleans. Called Clinical Pastoral Education, the experience is designed to help future priests and ministers to better serve those who are ill and hospitalized, to be more comfortable around sickness and death, and to gain deeper insight into how one's own personality and character shape ministry and engagement with others.

One day, my supervisor asked me to go visit a patient who was not on my floor (he had asked me if I wanted a special challenge, to which I said, "No, I feel challenged enough already," but he sent me anyway! Thank the Lord, as it all turned out later). This man, whom I will call Tom, had just suffered the suicide of his only son and a painful divorce from his wife, had just been diagnosed with AIDS as the result of drug abuse, and was about to be turned out of the hospital because he had no health insurance.

I had never knowingly met anyone with AIDS. I went in to greet him with much trepidation, as you can imagine. I told Tom who I was and that I was from the Pastoral Care department, to which he responded with curses, swearing, and a demand that I leave the room. Not a surprising response, given the situation. I somehow had the presence of mind to ask Tom if I could quietly sit in a chair in the corner for a few moments. I promised not to say anything. He told me to do what I pleased, but in more colorful language than that. I stayed for a minute, silently prayed for Tom, and then left. I repeated this for ten days.

On the eleventh day, Tom opened up, telling me the whole painful story of his life, filled with a lot of suffering, heartache, addictions, and emptiness. As he finished, we were both in tears. Then he asked me, "Do you think God could ever love and forgive me?" Without thinking about it, I hugged Tom, assuring him that God had never stopped loving him and that forgiveness was always possible. He told me later that it was the first time that someone had touched him without gloves since he had been diagnosed with AIDS. In that encounter, the Risen Lord touched both of us, a nervous seminarian and a broken, suffering man, bringing healing and peace.

I always think of that powerful experience on the second Sunday of Easter when chapter 20 of John's Gospel is proclaimed regarding the doubting Thomas. In John's narrative, Thomas comes to faith by touching the wounds of the Risen Christ, probing the nail marks and putting his hand into Jesus' wounded side. He comes to know that this mysterious and luminous figure in front of him is the same Jesus he knew in the flesh and who died on the Cross.

I often wondered why Jesus' wounds stubbornly remained after the Resurrection. After all, the mighty divine power that raised Jesus from the dead could certainly heal a few nail holes and a spear gash. Maybe the wounds stay to teach us that the victory of Easter Sunday doesn't completely obliterate the suffering of Good Friday, that even though Jesus has gained the victory over sin and death, we will still encounter suffering and darkness in this life, and that the story isn't quite finished, even though we know how it turns out in the end.

But now, through the power of the Resurrection, Jesus' wounds become trophies of victory, transformed into founts of mercy, healing, forgiveness, and love. Thomas comes to faith by touching them, and so do we. We touch the wounds of the Risen Lord every time we serve the poor, visit the sick, console the troubled, listen to a child, or reach out in love to a stranger. This truth is the great secret of the saints!

When Vincent de Paul, Mother Teresa, Camillus de Lellis, Louise de Marillac, and John of God loved the poor and served the distressed, they knew they were touching the very wounds of Christ! We are called to enter into the terrible suffering of this world with the light of Christ, to love the most neglected and marginalized courageously, and to unleash the powerful mercy of the Risen Christ by pouring ourselves out in service to others.

The Lord touched and healed me more than thirty years ago in a Louisiana hospital room, through a broken man who has been long dead, by inviting me to probe the nail holes and put my hand into His Sacred Side. I have never been fully the same since, for I was touched by the fire of the Divine Mercy.

Only a Few Steps

Back in 2011, I led a pilgrimage to the Holy Land with seminarians, an experience both beautiful and profound. Many spiritual commentators call Israel the "Fifth Gospel" because visiting the places made holy by the Lord's presence makes the life of Jesus come alive in living color. The highlight of the pilgrimage was visiting the Church of the Holy Sepulcher, which contains the place of both Jesus' Crucifixion and His Resurrection. I was surprised to learn that the place of Jesus' death was just a few steps away from His tomb, but it makes sense when you think of the logistics of burying those executed on that hill of death called "The Place of the Skull".

Just as only a few steps lead you from Golgotha to the Holy Sepulcher, so too Good Friday is only three days apart from Easter Sunday; only a few years separate us in this present moment from the glory of eternal life. To move from despair and pain to hope and new life only requires a fresh encounter with God now. Suffering and glory, pain and healing, sorrow and joy, darkness and light, are all so proximate to each other at times that they can get rolled up together; they can almost resemble each other in our human experience. John the Evangelist understood this well, for when he gazed upon the Crucified Jesus in all of that horror, he already saw the glory of God made manifest. Jesus crucified is already Jesus glorified.

When you suffer loss or pain, when darkness seems to have filled every corner of your soul, when God feels far away and silent, when Easter does not seem real, remember it is only a few steps from the Cross to the Resurrection, only a few days from Good Friday to Easter Sunday, only a few years from now to eternal life, only a blink of an eye before the Lord will show His merciful face again.

In God's timelessness, two thousand years is just a nanosecond, so wasn't it just the day before yesterday that Mary Magdalene ran down the path breathlessly to tell the dazed Apostles that the tomb was empty? Didn't Pentecost, in all the fiery power of the Holy Spirit, just happen a couple of hours ago? Let the eternal youth of God and the Church rejuvenate your spirit. The mission is just beginning, and we are a part of it.

The God of Surprises

I have always been struck by the fact that Jesus' closest friends failed to recognize Him in His Easter appearances. Mary Magdalene thinks Jesus is the gardener, the disciples on the road to Emmaus view Him as a fellow wayfarer, and the Apostles assume He is a ghost. What does this failure to see the Lord signify? Why don't the people who knew Jesus the best realize it is Him?

Could it be that their grief and sorrow blinded them from realizing that Jesus was in their midst? No one expected the Lord miraculously to rise from the dead, even though He had told them so. Because the rational expectations of Simon Peter, Mary Magdalene, and the others did not include the amazing possibility that they would ever see Jesus again, they didn't see Him, even when He was standing right in front of them.

What a great lesson is here for us. Oftentimes, I expect God to act, speak, and be present in particular ways, usually how I want Him to be God in my life. I have a predetermined bias of where, when, and how I will meet the Lord. All of the time, God eludes, transcends, and shatters my puny expectations! How often I fail to recognize the presence of the Lord in suffering, failure, frustration, or the seemingly ordinary. I am blind to the divine presence because God spoke and acted through a painful situation, an embarrassing failure, or a difficult person. The

Resurrection narratives teach us to expect God to surprise, shock, and even astonish us, by appearing unbidden, simultaneously in the strangest of places and the most ordinary of circumstances.

The Easter Gospels teach us the Risen Christ is neither just an incorporeal spirit nor a resuscitated body. Thomas touches the wounds of Jesus, the Lord eats a piece of fish in front of His friends, and He makes breakfast for the Apostles on the shore of Lake Tiberias. These incidents show that indeed the Lord Jesus rose from the dead in His human body and the tomb was empty. This truth is central to our Christian faith, for it signifies our fleshly human existence has been redeemed through the death and Resurrection of Christ. Salvation is not only about what happens to us in the next life, as absolutely important as eternal life with God is. The Lord wants us to live the abundance of His risen love now, in all aspects of our humanity. Easter is about our final destiny but also informs and inspires what we do in the next ten minutes.

The fact that the rising of Jesus is both physical and spiritual points to the integrity of the human person as an incarnate spirit; we are not just souls trapped in the prison of a body. Salvation in Christ transforms and affects all aspects of our life in this world; this conviction leads the Catholic Church to feed, house, educate, heal, and help more people on this planet than any other institution around. Because of the Resurrection of Christ, we are servants of the dignity of the human person, and the Gospel has economic, political, cultural, and social implications.

In His public ministry, Jesus raised the daughter of Jairus, the son of the widow of Naim, and Lazarus from the dead. As astounding as these miracles were, Jesus' own Resurrection is something altogether different. When He leaves the tomb, the Lord does not simply return to His previous earthly life. He appears and disappears at will, shows up behind locked doors, and does not remain in one place very long. In this glorified new life, culminating in the Ascension, Christ now has a radical and profound relationship with the entire universe, the human race, and the Church. He has lifted up all of creation to the Father in the singular act of redemption that we call the Paschal Mystery.

The Lord is now present in His Mystical Body, in the sacraments, particularly the Eucharist, in every heart touched by sanctifying grace, and in the poor, sick, and suffering. This glorified presence of Christ points to our own future glorification in the Kingdom of Heaven, where the just will shine like the sun, our own bodies will be transformed, and we will know the eternal bliss of life with God.

Pentecost Shake-Up

Each spring we celebrate the glorious Feast of Pentecost, the day when the Holy Spirit descended in wind and flame upon those gathered in the Upper Room with the Blessed Virgin Mary. How I would love to have been a fly on the wall that morning! What happened up there? What did the Apostles see and feel when the Holy Spirit filled them? We don't know for sure, but we can certainly see the difference that Pentecost makes.

When they enter the Upper Room, those first followers of Jesus are afraid, confused, and silent about their experience of the Risen Christ and not sure what to do next. Simon Peter wants to go back to fishing; it is the steady living that he knows. When they emerge from that room, they are transformed, courageous, united, on fire, confident, and articulate in their proclamation of the Crucified and Risen Christ as the new meaning of human history. Simon Peter, who ran away from the Cross and denied his Lord, is the one who now looks Jesus' killers in the eye and calls them to repentance, conversion, and Baptism. So spiritually explosive was that moment that three thousand

This is a modified version of an article previously published as "Outpouring of the Holy Spirit Calls Us to Live the Mission of Jesus", *Northwest Indiana Catholic* (website), accessed September 15, 2020, https://www.nwicatholic.com /index.php/2011-10-28-15-52-16/bishop-hying-column/2871-outpouring-of -the-holy-spirit-calls-us-to-live-the-mission-of-jesus.

people were baptized, and so the Church was born in this outpouring of the Holy Spirit.

While the Ascension marks the end of Jesus' earthly ministry, Pentecost is the beginning of our mission as members of the Church. The Lord anoints us in the power of the Holy Spirit, so that we can proclaim the Gospel to every creature, teach and preach, serve and heal, love and forgive. I am afraid that if Pentecost happened today, instead of immediately going out to evangelize, the early Church would have formed a long-range study committee, wrote up plans on how to evangelize, and organized countless meetings. Thankfully, they did none of that!

Instead, they went out into the streets and immediately started sharing their faith in and experience of Jesus Christ with every person they met. "Let me tell you about this man whom I came to know as the Son of God and the Lord of life!" Our tradition tells us that Peter ends up in Rome, Thomas goes to India, James to Spain, and Mary Magdalene travels to France—missionary journeys embraced in order to proclaim the saving Gospel of Jesus Christ.

When you hold your smartphone, you probably have more technology in your hand than Houston did when men landed on the moon in 1969. Amazing! Yet, if the battery is dead and you have no place to plug in, it doesn't make any difference. All of that powerful capacity is thoroughly out of reach. So it is with the Holy Spirit. The third Person of the Most Blessed Trinity is the love generated between the Father and the Son who pours forth the power, energy, animation, and inspiration to complete the mission of Jesus. We cannot pray, love, forgive, or say that Jesus is Lord except in the power of the Holy Spirit. Confirmation is our experience of Pentecost when the Lord anoints us in His Spirit so that we can live out our vocation as adopted children of the Father.

Are we living the mission of Jesus Christ or just maintaining institutions? Do we put more energy and resources into living the Good News or keeping up buildings? Do we just serve the people who come to us, or do we seek out those who are alienated and lost?

The Catholic Church is two thousand years old, a mammoth spread over the face of the earth, with more than a billion members. We need parishes, schools, hospitals, homeless shelters, formation centers, money, vehicles, personnel, and a plethora of resources to keep it all going. But like any institution, the Church runs the danger of turning in on herself, maintaining organizations, activities, and structures that no longer serve the mission and becoming complacent and tired.

Pentecost shakes us up. We need constantly to seek the anointing of the Holy Spirit so that we remain true to the mission of the Church, which is both simple and profound. Go, preach the Gospel to every creature, and make disciples in the name of the Lord Jesus. As we celebrate the birth of the Church, pray to the Holy Spirit and then do something outside of your comfort zone. Offer to pray with someone when they share a sorrow with you. Volunteer to take Communion to the homebound. Help out at a homeless shelter. Reach out to someone who is angry at you. Tell your family how much you love them.

Divine Fire

We give thanks and praise to God for the gift of the Holy Spirit! Jesus promises to send another Advocate—the Paraclete, the Consoler—to continue the mission of salvation, to breathe wisdom, energy, and holiness over the early Church, to teach the fullness of Jesus to the people until the end of time. As the living and eternal fruit of the love between the Father and the Son, the Holy Spirit is perpetually generated and active in the Church and the world.

I always like to think of the Holy Spirit as the fire, energy, and inspiring force of God who gets things done. In the book of Genesis, the Spirit breathes over the waters of creation; subsequently, the Spirit stirs up the hearts and words of the prophets, overshadows the Virgin Mary when she conceives Jesus, and anoints the Lord at His Baptism. Christ breathes the Holy Spirit on His Apostles the night of Easter and sends the fullness of the Advocate on the morning of Pentecost. We believe the Holy Spirit inspired the authors of the Scriptures to write the Word of God, and we invoke the third Person of the Trinity in every celebration of every sacrament. Just as your smartphone

This is a modified version of an article originally published as "Holy Spirit Is the Fire, Energy and Inspiring Force of God in Our Lives", *Northwest Indiana Catholic* (website), May 15, 2016, https://www.nwicatholic.com/index.php /2011-10-28-15-52-16/bishop-hying-column/3629-holy-spirit-is-the-fire -energy-and-inspiring-force-of-god-in-our-lives.

is of no use if the battery is dead, so too our faith, good works, and proclamation of the Gospel are fruitless unless the Spirit breathes life into us.

Various obstacles can get in the way of our faith. Fear of rejection or the opinion of others can keep us silent when we should be witnessing to the love of Christ. Laziness or tepidness sometimes prevents us from being zealous, ardent, and sacrificial in the love of God and neighbor. Anger at God, resentments toward others, or deep hurts from the past can build a wall that blocks us off from grace and leaves us in a lonely place.

Maybe somebody in the Church hurt or rejected us in the past. Being too busy with everything else can blind us to the absolute priority that God should hold in our lives.

We could define all of these challenges as spiritual artery blockages or hard-heartedness. Just as a person with serious obstructions in the arteries of the heart needs emergency surgery to place stents in the closed places and open up the flow of blood and life, so too we Christians need the Divine Physician—Jesus—to perform heart surgery on us.

When we open ourselves to the power of the Holy Spirit, through prayer and sacrament, the fire and grace of God can break down all of the walls, fear, anger, and laziness that keep us from dynamically growing toward discipleship and sainthood.

Before they received the power of the Holy Spirit, those first followers of Jesus were confused, silent about their experience of the Resurrection, fearful, divided, and not sure what to do next. In an instant, the fiery Spirit of God burned away all of their doubt and torpor, sending them out, first into Jerusalem and then later the whole world, to bear witness to the Good News.

Once they had drunk of the Spirit, they never looked back, gladly spending the rest of their lives extending the mission of Jesus Christ and courageously dying for their faith. The Holy Spirit is to the soul what breath is to the body. Without the Paraclete, we are spiritually dead.

My deepest prayer is that we will intensively and regularly pray to the Holy Spirit, asking for the Divine Fire to burn away all of the obstacles, difficulties, and divisions that prevent us from fully living our Catholic faith—to melt any hard-heartedness, to open the blocked arteries.

As we look at our political, economic, and sociological challenges that seem enormous at times, we profoundly need the courage, passion, joy, and generosity that the first disciples of Jesus and thousands of saints since have lived so effectively.

We must petition the Lord to pour out the fruits of the Holy Spirit on our parishes, schools, families, children, workplaces, communities, prisons, and hospitals, as well as on our priests, religious, deacons, lay ecclesial ministers, catechists, and bishops (boy, do I need it!).

All for Christ! All in the Holy Spirit! All glory to the Father!

Mary Stands at the Heart of the Paschal Mystery

We Catholics honor the Blessed Virgin Mary with extra devotion and love in the month of May. Rosary processions, May crownings, and special Marian altars express our gratitude and affection for the Mother of God as we celebrate the beauty of spring. In May, we also mark the feasts of Pentecost and the Visitation, two key moments in the life of Mary and the unfolding of our salvation through Christ and the Church.

While we do not worship Mary as God (as some people accuse us of doing), we do venerate her profoundly as the greatest saint ever. Why is Mary so important to us? The most obvious reason is her unique and indispensable role as the mother of Jesus. Mary gives flesh to the Word of God; through her, the invisible God becomes visible, the divine embraces the human, the Creator is now a creature, and the Lord enters the world. The Council of Ephesus bestowed the title *Theotokos* or "God-Bearer" upon the Virgin; she is the sacred portal through which

This is a modified version of an article originally published as "Mary Continues to Play a Unique and Indispensable Role as Mother of God", *Northwest Indiana Catholic* (website), accessed September 16, 2020, https://www.nwi catholic.com/index.php/2011-10-28-15-52-16/bishop-hying-column/2835 -mary-continues-to-play-a-unique-and-indispensable-role-as-mother-of-god.

God enters into our humanity. Without Mary, we do not have Jesus. It is that simple and that profound.

Mary's maternity is predicated on her discipleship—the faith, love, and surrender that led her to embrace the startling invitation of the Archangel Gabriel to become the Mother of God. She is the first and greatest Christian disciple, the original believer who places faith and obedience in the Word of God, even as she conceives and bears that Word within her very flesh. In the context of the entire trajectory of Jesus' life, Mary spent more time with Him than anybody else, nurturing, teaching, and forming the Lord through all the hidden years of Nazareth.

Mary was present in the key moments of Christ's life: His conception, birth, childhood, first miracle at Cana, the Crucifixion, and Pentecost. She says little in the Scriptures, but her presence speaks volumes about her mediating and prayerful role in the ministry and mission of her Son. In chapter 2 of John's Gospel, at the marriage at Cana, Jesus calls Mary "woman", which sounds rather rude to our ears until we understand that He is speaking theologically. Mary is the new Eve, the new woman who brings grace, life, and hope to the human race through her fiat, just as Eve had ushered in sin and death. Similarly, Christ is the new Adam, the new man whose obedience negates the Original Sin of the first man.

We honor Mary's faith, for she believed two humanly impossible mysteries and staked her life on their truth. She embraced the words of the angel and so conceived the Son of God in her womb, and at the foot of the Cross, she trusted in the Resurrection of Jesus, standing as a beacon of hope and light in the bloody Hell of Golgotha. Spiritually, she shared fully in the Passion and death of the Lord, as only a mother's heart and soul could.

In my office hangs a print of a beautiful altarpiece painted by Roger Van der Weyden during the Flemish Renaissance, which depicts the Descent from the Cross. In this magnificent work, Mary imitates her Son. Jesus is dead; Mary has fainted. Both are drained of color and life. The motion and angle of their bodies are parallel, as Jesus is taken down from the Cross and Mary falls unconscious to the ground. This artistic symmetry communicates the deep theological truth that Mary shared fully in the death of her Son and so stands at the very heart of the Paschal Mystery, as a witness, a martyr, an intercessor, a model for our own faith, and a path of crucified love.

All of the saints had a tender and deep devotion to the Mother of God, for they intuited correctly that she would unerringly lead them to the depth of Christ's heart and life. The Scriptures tell us repeatedly that Mary stored her rich and beautiful experiences of Jesus in her heart, contemplating the wonder of God made flesh in her life. When we pray the Rosary, are we not asking Mary to open the storehouse of her heart and to share with us the treasured fruit of her contemplation? The Rosary is a sure, simple, and profound method of prayer that leads us to ponder the central mysteries of our faith and to be led to a deeper relationship with Jesus.

During my childhood, my family prayed the Rosary every night after supper, 365 days a year. I must confess there were days I would have preferred to be playing outside, but looking back now, that discipline of prayer planted the faith deeply in my heart and led me to the priesthood.

As we honor Mary during the beautiful month of May or anytime, we ask her to intercede for us and to teach us her path of radical discipleship.

ALL SAINTS' DAY

Go for Broke—Become a Saint

I have always been fascinated with the saints because they show us what holiness looks like in so many varied and inspiring forms. They are to the spiritual life what astronauts are to outer space; the saints explore the uncharted territory of God's love, grace, and mercy.

When people called Dorothy Day, the founder of the Catholic Worker Movement and a person radically dedicated to peace and to the poor, a saint, she famously replied, "I don't want to be dismissed that easily."[1] She has a point. Oftentimes we do not consider the saints to be truly human or like us; the accounts of their lives often read like a superheroes comic book or appear almost mythological. Yet, Christ and the Church call us to become saints—in other words, to grow gradually into being the person that God has called us to become, to embrace the dream of a life radically surrendered to love.

Although this thinking was never the official teaching of the Church, the popular understanding of sanctity saw

This is a modified version of an article previously published as "World Always in Needs of Saints to Point Us toward God as a Common Goal", *Northwest Indiana Catholic* (website), accessed September 16, 2020, https://www.nwicatholic.com/index.php/2011-10-28-15-52-16/bishop-hying-column/3218-world-always-in-needs-of-saints-to-point-us-toward-god-as-a-common-goal.

[1]David Van Bierna, "Candidate Saints: Dorothy Day", Rhythm of the Saints, *Time*, accessed January 8, 2021, http://content.time.com/time/specials/packages/article/0,28804,1850894_1850895_1850863,00.html.

it as the preserve of priests, nuns, and monks. If you really wanted to be holy, you embraced priesthood or religious life; marriage, family, and the world of the laity was for everybody else. The documents of Vatican II powerfully remind us that everyone is called to be a saint by virtue of Baptism; we need holy married couples, parents, teachers, chefs, doctors, and factory workers.

Saint Francis de Sales foreshadowed this shift by centuries when he wrote in his *Introduction to the Devout Life* that it would be absurd for a mother of five to live the spirituality of a cloistered nun or for a merchant to pray in the same way as a priest. The dual canonization of Zelie and Louis Martin, the parents of Saint Thérèse of Lisieux, reflects the importance of lifting up saintly role models for laypeople.

Since my childhood, the lives of the saints have fascinated me! The joyful drama of Francis of Assisi giving away all his possessions, serving the poor, and receiving the stigmata inspired me. The unique and brief trajectory of Joan of Arc's mysterious life and mission intrigued me. The extraordinary priesthood of John Vianney, who tirelessly heard confessions for sixteen hours a day, overwhelmed me. The passionate love of Saint Thérèse of Lisieux, lived out in the ordinary details of life, beckoned me.

The saints show us that it is literally possible to live the teachings of Jesus in such a totally generous way that we become a new creation in Christ. As Saint Paul says, "It is no longer I who live but, Christ who lives in me."[2] The saints become living icons of the Gospel, as the Word of God is imbedded and manifest in the conversion and spirituality of their lives.

So what unites personalities and temperaments as different as Philip Neri, known for his humor and jokes, and

---

[2] Gal 2:20.

Jerome, who was irascible; Julian of Norwich, who never left her one-room cell, and Francis Xavier, who traveled the Far East; Thomas Aquinas, a philosophical genius, and Joseph of Cupertino, who struggled with the books? Each saint heard the call of God, experienced the pulsating love of the divine, and eventually surrendered every facet of their lives and personalities to the Lord. They fell in love with Jesus Christ, and nothing could ever be the same again. This spiritual movement toward integrity is the challenge and joy of the journey toward conversion.

Every Gothic cathedral in Europe has a rose window, an artistic explosion of glass and light composed of concentric circles of figures. Jesus Christ is always at the center of the window; the next circle pictures the Apostles; the third one depicts various saints; and the outer circles represent the world of work, animals, nature, and the details of medieval life.[3]

The lesson of the rose window is one of integrity. If Christ is truly at the center of life, then everyone and everything revolve in a beautiful harmony around that center in love, justice, and peace. The window symbolizes the well-ordered life, both individual and communal, in which family, work, politics, economics, sexuality, friendship, learning, leisure, money, and time all fit together in a harmonious whole and find their ultimate purpose in the truth, beauty, and goodness of God.

The world will always need saints, joyous and generous women and men who point us beyond the ephemeral things of this world to God as our ultimate goal and good;

[3] Bishop Robert Barron, "Bishop Barron on Making Christ the Center of Your Life", *Word on Fire Blog*, February 17, 2017, https://www.wordon fire.org/resources/blog/bishop-barron-on-making-christ-the-center-of-your -life/2242/.

we, too, are called to be radical and passionate witnesses who reject the false values of selfishness, comfort, and complacency to show everyone that the only reason every human being is alive, the only purpose for which we exist, is to fall head over heels in love with God and to draw as many people as we can into the divine romance that will last forever!

As Saint Irenaeus said seventeen hundred years ago, the glory of God is the human being fully alive. Go for broke—become a saint. We only get to live this life once.

Death: The Sweet Portal

As we approach the end of October, we observe nature surrendering to the annual cycle of death. Leafless trees, harvested fields, shorter days, and cold nights point to the slow and steady creep of winter's grasp. The liturgy of the Church embraces this mystery as well. In November, we pray for and remember the dead, the readings for Mass speak of the end of the world, and we reflect on the final judgment as we come once again to the end of the liturgical year on the Feast of Christ the King (the last Sunday before the first Sunday of Advent). The Church invites us to meditate on the brevity of this life, the mystery of death, and the promise of eternity.

One of the most significant events in my life was the death of my brother Patrick. Born on Saint Patrick's Day, 1959, he contracted liver cancer at the age of ten and died on November 26, 1969, the day after my mother's birthday and the day before Thanksgiving. Some people assume that children do not understand death; I beg to differ. I remember Patrick's illness and passing as if it happened the day before yesterday.

This is a modified version of an article previously published as "Paschal Mystery Show Us the Way through Death into God's Light and Joy", *Northwest Indiana Catholic* (website), accessed September 16, 2020, https://www.nwicatholic.com/index.php/2011-10-28-15-52-16/bishop-hying-column/3214-fall.

Going through my own sorrow and watching my parents grieve up close as a six-year-old forever marked my heart and life. A strange and sad emptiness entered our family and our house. I remember one day at dinner, my father stood up and took the empty chair that Patrick had always sat in out of the kitchen; it did not return for many years. Our sorrow and loss as a family gradually healed through faith, prayer, and the kindness of family and friends, but the experience both wounded and transformed us.

All of us, as mortal human beings, face the certainty of death, that of our loved ones and our own passing. From the moment we are born, we steadily move toward that guaranteed moment when our heart will stop beating and our final breath exhales, as we pass over from this life, never to return.

We fear death as the great unknown; we resent death as a robber and destroyer; we fight death as the enemy of all we know ourselves and the world to be. We experience death as profoundly unnatural, and so we should. It doesn't feel like part of God's plan for us. The book of Genesis, chapter 3, views death as the fruit of sin, as the ultimate consequence of humanity's choice to turn away from the life-giving relationship with God that sustains all things in breath and being.

The astonishing good news of our faith in Christ is that God carves a path for us through the tragedy of death by sending us Jesus. By accepting our sin and by submitting Himself to our death on that terrible Cross, Jesus embraces everything that is empty, evil, dark, and dead within us, and then through the greatest act of self-oblation, He lifts it all to the Father.

The Resurrection of Christ from the dead becomes the Father's response to this radical sacrificial gift offered by the Son. When the centurion pierces the side of the Crucified Christ, blood and water flow out, symbolizing the torrent of mercy and forgiveness that we most profoundly encounter in the water of Baptism and the Body and Blood of the Eucharist.

Life conquers death; mercy overpowers sin; love transforms hatred. God suffers with us, dies with us, and ultimately rises for us. The shocking mercy of God leads us through the pain, dread, and loneliness of the valley of death into the communion, light, and joy of the eternal Kingdom of Heaven. The Paschal Mystery does not magically remove suffering and death from our human experience, but shows us a way through and out of it. There is light at the end of the tunnel!

In his beautiful Canticle of the Sun, Francis of Assisi names the sun and the moon, the wind and the stars, fire and water, the earth and all creatures, as brother and sister. He even includes a verse honoring Sister Death; this great saint who learned to die radically to self and hand his whole being over to the Lord of Life had, in the end, befriended his mortality; for Francis, death was the sweet portal through which we enter to meet God and enjoy the divine embrace forever. How liberating and peaceful it is to sit with someone who has wrestled with the angel of death and come to terms with it! Such a person exudes a tranquility that is not of this world.

We need to pray for all of the deceased members of our parishes and families with particular attention and love. We pray for all those mourning the loss of a loved one. We ask the Lord to console and strengthen us in the deep conviction that death does not have the final word on our lives and that we will live forever with God.

As painful as it was, my brother's death blessed me. This tragic experience opened me to ask the big questions and brought me to a richer faith, gave me a deeper compassion for the suffering of others, and gained for me a powerful intercessor in Heaven. In many ways, I feel that my vocation to the priesthood was nurtured by the tragic death of Patrick. He has prayed and loved me to the place where I am.